THE ULTIMATE
GUYS' BODY BOOK

D0047913

What the experts are saying about
The Ultimate Guys' Body Book

Dr. Walt addresses "the talk" with wisdom and a sense of humor.

Kent Petrie, MD
Assistant Clinical Professor of Family Medicine,
University of Colorado Health Sciences Center

The Ultimate Guys' Body Book is the most practical and thoroughly biblical book that I've ever read for boys. It provides help, hope, and understanding.

Dr. Sammy Tippit, President
Sammy Tippit Ministries
Author and International Christian Conference Speaker

This will be a book that I'll strongly recommend to the Christian parents of pre- and young adolescents—as a guide for them to use in helping their male teen navigate these difficult years.

Joseph Zanga, MD, FAAP, FCP
Past President, American College of Pediatricians
Chief of Pediatrics, Columbus Regional Healthcare System

At a time when the nation's moral conscience has been seared, this book will provide a righteous GPS for the next generation of young men! Dr. Larimore exposes all the elephants in the room we all are too timid to talk about!

Gerald R. Parsons, MDiv
Senior Pastor, Covenant Life Church

... Provides practical, usable insight into the challenges faced by every boy navigating the intimidating pathway to becoming a man. Dr. Larimore's exceptional medical wisdom and deep compassion make him an excellent guide for this journey. I wholeheartedly recommend this book.

David P. Armentrout, PhD
Psychologist and Director of Behavioral Medicine
In His Image Family Medicine Residency Program

The Ultimate Guys' Body Book provides a perfect springboard to launch into the pool of puberty with your maturing young man. This biblically sound and scientifically accurate resource is a must-have in every Christian parent's bookshelf! While very readable and understandable, Dr. Larimore does not shy away from those difficult topics that befuddle so many adolescent boys—and their dads! It opened wonderful times of heart-to-heart discussion with my nearly teen son.

*J. Scott Ries, MD
Family Physician and National Director,
Campus & Community Ministries
Christian Medical and Dental Associations*

This book could make the difference between a young man choosing to believe God's grace-filled view of himself instead of the world's warped view. I highly recommend parents read *The Ultimate Guys' Body Book* with their sons when they reach those critical preteen years, before hormonal and societal pressures threaten to distort the truth.

Robert P. Vogt, MD

I recommend every parent, youth pastor, and counselor get a copy of this book. This essential guide ... will help build a sense of purpose, dignity, and positive expectation during their growing years—instead of fear, guilt, and confusion. It provides common-sense answers to important questions ... while including warmth, humor, and understanding.

*Carrie Abbott
President, The Legacy Institute*

Dr. Larimore consistently provides clinically sound, biblically based insight and guidance on many topics.... Parents, physicians, and youth groups will do well to include this guide as a cornerstone for young men coming of age. Read, talk, and be blessed!

Adam L. Myers, MD, CHCQM, CPHRM
Senior Vice President, Chief Medical Officer, Methodist Health System

Teen boys wrestle with doubt, anxiety, and enormous peer pressure. Dr. Walt has written a book that addresses the many questions guys have about that awkward, painful time of life. He offers boys trustworthy advice in a candid, approachable style. His coaching and encouragement in *The Ultimate Guys' Body Book* will take the sting out of those difficult adolescent years!

John Fuller
Christian Radio Broadcaster

... Dr. Larimore's forwardness and honesty in dealing with "taboo" subjects are so refreshing and so needed.

Jacob M. Wood, MD

The issues are tough and the temptations are great, but Dr. Larimore boldly addresses them within the context of the Christian faith. *The Ultimate Guys' Body Book* is an indispensible resource for parents as they raise boys in a world of challenges.

Pastor Robert Fleischmann
National Director, Christian Life Resources

As a family physician and father of six (three boys), I understand the vital need for the information Dr. Walt is sharing .... In a world flooded with misinformation and confusion regarding these issues, Dr. Walt has given all of us an incredibly useful tool for teaching our sons about growing up, and God's plans and purposes for each of us.

Mitchell W. Duininck, MD, FAAFP

President, In His Image, Inc.
Program Director, In His Image Family Medicine Residency

Most parents don't talk to their sons about the many changes that happen to a boy's body during puberty, so guys often get a lot of bad information from all the wrong places. Dr. Walt Larimore has solved that problem with *The Ultimate Guys' Body Book*—a gut-level, honest book that will protect boys from embarrassment as they grow into confident young men. I highly recommend it.

Dwight Bain
Founder of the LifeWorks Group
Nationally Certified Counselor & Certified Life Coach

Finally, a book for our young men that is informative, medically accurate, and biblically sound, yet written in a way that appeals to teens. Dr. Walt has skillfully addressed even the most sensitive issues that are bombarding our youth, but are rarely discussed ... from a Christian worldview. A great resource!

Susan Henriksen, MD

As the father of an older teenage boy, I wish this book had been available a few years earlier. It would have helped some awkward discussions and with dispelling some misperceptions my son learned from his friends.

David Flower, MA
Founder/President, Christian Development Fund

The Ultimate Guys' Body Book is not only great for early adolescents to read, but is also a "must-have" resource for dads and moms to help guide their teenage sons through these often turbulent years hormonally, physically, emotionally, culturally, and spiritually.

Paul R. Williams, MD, FAAP
Pediatrician

Visiting Faculty at In His Image Family Medicine Residency Program
Former Associate Professor of Pediatrics at University of South Florida

In this book Dr. Larimore answers the questions every guy wants to know but without having to face the embarrassment of asking. It will also help parents provide answers to questions they may not know how to answer.

John V. Thomas
Senior Pastor, King of Kings Baptist Church, and Founder, Living Hope

Dr. Larimore is able to encapsulate the questions on the hearts of young men. He speaks to their concerns and observations about adolescent changes. He helps young men feel comfortable as they mature physically, emotionally, and spiritually.

Mary Nelson, MD, DABFP
Family Physician

… A practical and enjoyable read for parents and their sons. It wouldn't surprise me if the parents learned as much as the sons.

Ed Dawson, MS
Clinical Psychologist
Engaging Life Psychological Services

Addresses with expertise, honesty, and transparency many topics that matter to our teens. Well-researched and full of practical wisdom, this book confronts tough questions with biblical truth to guide teens to godly living. Thank you, Dr. Walt, for equipping and challenging our sons as they grow into men whose lives make a difference.

Amaryllis Sánchez Wohlever, MD

As a father of two sons and a pastor for thirty-five years, I think this book would have been immeasurably helpful. I do not feel that I did an adequate job in this area with my two sons or as a pastor-equipper. This material, grounded in good biblical understanding and enhanced with solid medical knowledge and experience, will be an extremely valuable resource. I intend to recommend it often.

Larry E. Miller, DMin
Founder and President, Equippers Ministry

An extremely useful resource for preteen boys, their parents, and their doctors. Walt Larimore has hit the nail right on the head!

Ed Guttery, MD, FAAP, FCP

Dr. Walt Larimore has addressed issues on which little has been written for fathers and sons ... in a biblical manner. I am very grateful for his work and am sure that it will be a blessing to many.

Rodney Wood, DMin
Founder and President, The Mission Foundation

... Well-written, accurate, and timely....

Leanna Lindsey Hollis, MD

... A great tool to help parents and preteen boys discuss the most important issues they face on their journeys to manhood.... Medically accurate ... theologically sound ... accessible and interesting to this age group.

Laurel Williston, MD
Associate Professor of Family Medicine, In His Image Family Medicine
Residency

God has used Dr. Walt to teach and encourage about the tough adolescent issues faced by young men in today's sex-saturated society. I consider this a must-read for any parent, teacher, or coach who cares about boys.

Dean Patton, MD
Professor of Family Medicine, University of East Carolina School of
Medicine

Another great book from Dr. Walt—biblical, educational, and fun to read! ... I can't wait to recommend it to my patients and my own son!

Julian T. Hsu, MD
Assistant Clinical Professor of Family Medicine, University of Colorado
Health Sciences Center

Growing from boyhood to manhood takes a long time. You should spend some of it reading this book.

Donald Nelson, MD
Clinical Assistant Professor, Department of Family Medicine, University
of Iowa College of Medicine

... Countless insights that will be indispensable to young men who want to know how God made them and why.

Brian Duignan, MD

Other Books by Walt Larimore, MD

Nonfiction

Lintball Leo's Not-So-Stupid Questions About Your Body
(coauthored with John Riddle, illustrated by Mike Phillips)

*10 Essentials of Happy, Healthy People:
Becoming and Staying Highly Healthy*

Alternative Medicine: The Christian Handbook
(coauthored with Doìnal O'Mathuìna)

*SuperSized Kids: How to Rescue Your Child
from the Obesity Threat*
(coauthored with Cheryl Flynt and Steve Halliday)

Why A.D.H.D. Doesn't Mean Disaster
(coauthored with Dennis Swanberg and Diane Passno)

*His Brain, Her Brain: How Divinely Designed
Differences Can Strengthen Your Marriage*
(coauthored with Barbara Larimore)

*The Honeymoon of Your Dreams:
A Practical Guide to Planning a Romantic Honeymoon*
(coauthored with Susan A. Crockett)

*Bryson City Tales: Stories of a Doctor's
First Year of Practice in the Smoky Mountains*

*Bryson City Seasons: More Tales of a Doctor's
Practice in the Smoky Mountains*

*Bryson City Secrets: Even More Tales of a
Small-Town Doctor in the Smoky Mountains*

Workplace Grace: Becoming a Spiritual Influence at Work
(coauthored with William Carr Peel)

*Workplace Grace: Becoming a Spiritual Influence at Work —
Groupware™ Curriculum, with video, DVD, leader's guide,
and participant's workbook*

*The Saline Solution: Becoming a Spiritual Influence in Your
Medical Practice, small-group curriculum with DVD, leader's
guide, and participant's workbook*
(coauthored with William Carr Peel)

Fiction

Time Series Investigators: The Gabon Virus

Time Series Investigators: The Influenza Bomb (coauthored
with Paul McCusker)

Hazel Creek

Sugar Fork

Dr. Walt's health website is www.DrWalt.com.
Dr. Walt's blog is www.DrWalt.com/blog.
Purchase additional titles and autographed books from Dr. Walt at
http://dr-walts-store.hostedbyamazon.com.

Not-So-Stupid Questions
About Your Body

THE ULTIMATE GUYS' BODY BOOK

Dr. Walt Larimore

ZONDER**kidz**

ZONDERVAN.com/
AUTHORTRACKER
follow your favorite authors

ZONDERKIDZ

The Ultimate Guys' Body Book
Copyright © 2012 by Dr. Walt Larimore

Illustrations © 2012 by (Illustrator Name or Zonderkidz Here)

This title is also available as a Zondervan ebook.
Visit www.zondervan.com/ebooks

Requests for information should be addressed to:

Zonderkidz, *Grand Rapids, Michigan 49530*

Library of Congress Cataloging-in-Publication Data

Larimore, Walter L.
    The ULtimate Guys' Body Book : a Christian physician honestly answers
your questions about your body / Walt Larimore.
        p. cm.
    ISBN 978-0-310-72323-3 (softcover)
    1. Teenage boys — Physiology—Juvenile literature. 2. Teenage boys—Health
and hygiene—Juvenile literature. 3. Puberty—Juvenile literature. 4.
Adolescence—Juvenile literature. 5. Human growth—Juvenile literature.
6. Teenage boys—Sexual behavior—Juvenile literature. 7. Sex instruction
for boys—Religious aspects—Christianity—Juvenile literature. 8. Teenage
boys—Conduct of life—Juvenile literature. I. Title.
RJ143.L35 2012
    613'.04233—dc23   2011034992

Published in association with the literary agency of Alive Communications, Inc.
7680 Goddard Street, Suite 200, Colorado SPrings, CO 80920.

Zonderkidz is a trademark of Zondervan.

Art direction: Cindy Davis
Cover design: Cindy Davis
Interior Illustration: Guy Francis
Interior design: Matthew Van Zomeren

Printed in the United States of America

12 13 14 15 16 17 18 /DCI/ 20 19 18 17 16 15 14 13 12 11 10 9 8 7 6 5 4 3 2 1

To Scott
I've always been grateful to be your dad.
I always will be.

The father of a righteous child has great joy; a man who
fathers a wise son rejoices in him.   *Proverbs 23:24*

CONTENTS

NOTE TO PARENTS

The Ultimate Guys' Body Book is primarily written to be a resource for Christian parents, especially the dads of young men ages ten to thirteen years old. It's designed to help you answer your boy's tough questions about puberty and his changing body.

As a Christian family physician, I want you to have information you can trust—a handbook for you and your son that is both medically reliable and biblically sound. To accomplish this, I have:

1. Reviewed the latest research and national guidelines through the lens of a biblical worldview.
2. Had every chapter reviewed by researchers, physicians, dieticians, psychologists, coaches, pastors, educators, parents, and theologians, who are all listed at the back of the book.
3. Had the book reviewed by the Christian Medical Association.

This book is designed to assist you in one of the most important and difficult jobs you'll ever have—raising and nurturing a young man to become physically, emotionally, relationally, and spiritually healthy. Your son needs coaching and mentoring to help him through adolescence and puberty on his journey from childhood to tweendom to adulthood.

Boys need to be assured—particularly by their fathers (or male role models) — that issues like wet dreams, hair growth, mood changes, voice change, and sexual desire are part of this *normal* and divinely designed transition. This book will help you do that.

You can maximize the benefits of this book in a couple of ways:

Option 1: Read through the book quickly to get an overview *before* giving it to your son. You don't have to study the book; just skim through. If it looks appropriate, and if you think your son is mature enough for the information, give it to him to read. But if you choose this option, I recommend you keep tabs of where your son is in the book. Give him the time and opportunity to talk to you about any of the information he encounters as he is reading.

Option 2: I most highly recommend — particularly for dads — slowly reading and studying the book *with* your son. I can't tell you how many comments I've received from dads who used this option with my book *Lintball Leo's Not-So-Stupid Questions About Your Body*. Almost without exception, dads said that the quality time they spent with their sons was extremely valuable.

If you are a single mom and uncomfortable reading this with your son, (or think he may be uncomfortable reading it with you) then find a *trusted* male role model that you know well who might be willing to go through this information with your son — perhaps a youth pastor, coach, or the husband of a dear friend.

The key is that *The Ultimate Guys' Body Book* can help you connect with your son and allow you to reassure him that he will not be alone during these sometimes scary and confusing changes he is experiencing.

Also, it demonstrates to him that you will be there to coach him, support him, root for him, and protect him during his adolescent years. It lets him know he can come to you for truthful answers on *any* issues that concern him. After all, if he can't ask you, he's likely to ask someone else — and who knows what type of information he might get?

Whatever option you choose, don't worry if your son starts

asking questions you can't answer. Just say, "I don't know the answer. But let's see if we can find it together." Your son's physician, a coach at school, your pastor, or your son's youth pastor may all be excellent resources for more information.

When you are honest about what you know and what you don't know, you build bridges of communication and trust. You're telling your son that you are giving him the "real deal" about issues that are of critical importance to him.

Last but not least, be prepared to spend time praying, meditating, studying, and learning with your son. Give him and yourself time to absorb the material and think, talk, and pray together about it. My hope is when you and your son are finished, this book will be worn—and your efforts will be rewarded!

Another tip to consider is purchasing a journal to use as you and your son read this book. Write your name, your son's name, and the date you begin your journey on the first page. After you read a section of this book with your son, or after you have a talk with your son, record the discussions along with your feelings and thoughts. Your son may also benefit from using the journal to ask embarrassing questions in writing. If there is something your son wants to know but would rather not talk about, tell him to ask in the journal. You can offer to write back or talk openly. You can also write back-and-forth to let each other know when you're upset or angry without being confrontational. This method has proven invaluable opening new avenues of communication and for helping some kids express their awkward feelings. This journal can be wonderful information to share later with your son as he grows and matures.

Most of all, plan to have fun as you begin this life-changing journey with your son.

> Train a child in the way he should go, and when he is old he will not turn from it. *Proverbs 22:6*

> Fathers ... bring [your children] up in the training and instruction of the Lord. *Ephesians 6:4*

NOTE TO YOUNG MEN

I'm on your side; I'm *your* fan; I believe in you.

You not only have your entire life in front of you, but as a young Christian—as a young man who is a follower of Jesus—you have a golden opportunity to change and improve the world.

"But I'm not old enough to change the world," you might say. "I'm too young to make a difference!" That is *not* the case. Decisions you make now and for the next few years will not only change the rest of your life, they could literally change eternity. Let me explain:

To change the world and to carry on his message, Jesus chose a group of young men to train who were close to your age. As you look at the gospels, you'll see that Jesus spoke to the crowds, but he seemed to give preference to smaller groups—including the twelve young men he chose for special training—out of which he picked three for advanced training.

Gunter Krallman, in his book *Mentoring for Mission*, points out that Jesus was a rabbi, and rabbis typically chose disciples who were between the ages of fourteen and sixteen. At the time of Jesus, Galilean boys typically married at age eighteen, and yet only Simon Peter was said to have been married.

The story of the temple tax also sheds some light on the ages of the disciples. According to the Old Testament (Exodus 30:14), this tax was due to the temple from all Hebrew males twenty and older. Yet in Matthew 17:24–25, after Jesus and his disciples arrived in

Capernaum, the collectors of the two-drachma temple tax came to Peter and asked, "Doesn't your teacher pay the temple tax?"

"Yes, he does," Peter replied.

Jesus then told Peter,

> "But so that we may not cause offense, go to the lake and throw out your line. Take the first fish you catch; open its mouth and you will find a four-drachma coin. Take it and give it to them for my tax and yours." *Matthew 17:26–27*

The other eleven disciples are with Jesus at this point, yet no mention is made of their provision. That makes it very likely that the other eleven disciples didn't owe the tax because they weren't yet twenty years old.

Therefore, it's likely that Jesus chose teenage boys—boys about your age, and the ages of your friends—to be his disciples and to change their world! Dr. Jeff Myers, the chairman of Summit Ministries agrees. He says, "These pieces of evidence are circumstantial, of course, but they point to an intriguing possibility: when Jesus Christ, God in the flesh, chose twelve ordinary males to change the world, he started with teenage boys." Or, as Gunter Krallman puts it, "Jesus wasn't just starting a movement—he was starting a youth movement."

In addition, God chose teenage boys throughout the Bible to change their culture and to change the world. God chose Isaac, Jacob, Moses, David, Jonathan, Solomon, Jeremiah, Samson, Daniel, Josiah, Isaiah, and Timothy. So the Bible gives us an impressive list of young men who knew what they believed, were committed to their Lord, and knew where they were going in life.

I believe there is a warrior inside every young man. If your generation of young men were to rise up to stand for truth and fight against evil and injustice—if you and your friends abandon a consumer-oriented, media-addicted, passive lifestyle—you will exert a tremendous influence on the world, for good and for Christ.

So in this book, I won't just talk about all of the physical changes you will be going through these next few years. I'll also address some spiritual issues. Why?

The Bible teaches that Satan will do everything he can to attack you on your journey through life. The Bible calls Satan and his fallen angels *liars* and *accusers*. Satan knows because you are God's child that you can be used by God to defeat him and his evil plans. Therefore, anything Satan can do to defeat you or lower you self-esteem (how you feel about yourself), he will do.

Remember that you are a child of God, made in his image. So to help you see God's divine design for your development, I'll share what God's Word says about many of your questions and add in some of my best medical advice.

It's been said, "Young men who stand for something are not likely to easily fall for just anything." Joseph beat sexual temptation. Daniel wouldn't compromise his integrity for a political promotion. Young King Josiah stood firm on ethics. David, as a young shepherd, showed exemplary courage in the face of danger. And the young apostles and Timothy were part of the greatest adventure of all—being followers of Jesus in the first century.

Paul wrote to his young disciple, Timothy:

> Don't let anyone look down on you because you are young, but set an example for the believers in speech, in conduct, in love, in faith and in purity. *1 Timothy 4:12*

However, and this is very important, I do not want you to underestimate the importance of your parents as you take this journey from boyhood to manhood. They are part of God's divine design to help you grow into a young man.

Therefore, I recommend that, whenever possible, you include your parents, especially your dad, as you read this book. If your dad is not available to you, then either talk to your mom or work with her to find a Christian man you both trust to help you with this journey—perhaps a pastor, youth pastor, teacher, scout master, coach, or someone else.

Now, I'm the first to admit that initially this i.
uncomfortable, but I believe it's critical. As Jesus said,

> "Moses gave you this law from God: 'Honor your father
> and mother,' and 'Anyone who speaks disrespectfully of
> father or mother must be put to death.'" *Mark 7:10 NLT*

My purpose in this book is to help you see yourself through
the eyes of your Creator and to help you understand that your
Creator has an amazing plan for you. Are you ready to begin? If
so, now's the time to take that first step—and it's my privilege to
be one of your coaches for this part of the journey.

But in case you're wondering how you can possibly change the
world when you're trying to deal with your changing voice, not to
worry. This book talks about a lot of the questions you and your
friends may have about your changing bodies and lives.

Also, let me encourage you *not* to skip the verses at the end of
each chapter. Rather, take some time to read them, think about
them, and let them settle in your heart.

> A wise son brings joy to his father, but a foolish son brings
> grief to his mother. *Proverbs 10:1*

> Listen to your father, who gave you life, and do not despise
> your mother when she is old. Buy the truth and do not sell
> it—get wisdom, instruction and insight as well.
> *Proverbs 23:22–23*

> Children, obey your parents in the Lord, for this is right.
> "Honor your father and mother"—which is the first com-
> mandment with a promise—"so that it may go well with
> you and that you may enjoy long life on the earth."
> *Ephesians 6:1–3*

> Children, obey your parents in everything, for this pleases
> the Lord. *Colossians 3:20*

QUESTION 1

I'm changing! What's happening to my body?

The word *puberty* is probably used a lot around you, right? But what does it mean? Here's my definition: puberty is the process that develops and changes your body physically from being a boy to being a man.

During puberty you will grow hair in new places, your private parts will become larger, your voice will become lower, and you will have new feelings and emotions. During puberty, your body will grow faster than at any other time in your life, except for when you were in your mother's womb or when you were a very tiny child.

It may seem weird or scary, but it is actually a normal, healthy, and God-designed process for your body.

All boys go through puberty at different ages and at different rates. Usually, puberty starts between the ages of ten to fifteen. If your puberty starts before ten or has not started by the time you turn fifteen, you should see your doctor.

Puberty begins when your brain releases a variety of different hormones. Hormones are chemicals made by a gland in one part of your body. During puberty, hormones are carried by the bloodstream to other parts of your body, where they cause specific effects.

In both boys and girls, the same exact hormones start the process of puberty (although it starts earlier for most girls). For boys and girls, these hormones go to work on different parts of the body. For us guys, these hormones give our testicles a chemical signal to begin making two things: sperm and testosterone.

Sperm are tiny cells made by the testicles. The male sperm helps create life (a baby) when it combines with an egg from a female. But more on that later.

Most of the changes in your body during puberty are caused by the hormone called testosterone. Combined with the "growth hormone" produced by the pituitary gland in the brain, testosterone causes you to grow taller and bigger. It causes your muscles to grow. It causes your body hair and genitals to grow. It changes your voice.

Although your Creator has designed the changes of puberty that lead to manhood, that doesn't mean that these adjustments aren't scary. They are, not only to you, but also to every boy who has ever gone through them.

So let's begin discussing some of these changes.

> Oh yes, you shaped me first inside, then out; you formed me in my mother's womb. I thank you, High God—you're breathtaking! Body and soul, I am marvelously made! I worship in adoration—what a creation
>
> *Psalm 139:13–15 MSG*

Amazing Bean

Small, bean shaped, and reddish gray, the pituitary gland looks like something that belongs in a burrito — not your brain. But it's actually one of the most important organs in your entire body, especially during puberty. Sometimes called "the master gland," the pituitary controls hormone functions that regulate your temperature, growth, and testosterone production.

Located near the base of your brain, the pituitary gland triggers puberty by signaling to your testicles to start producing more testosterone. It also controls how much growth hormone is released in your body. In rare occasions the pituitary puts out too much growth hormone before puberty when a person's long bones in the body are still growing. This causes gigantism, or extreme tallness.

According to Guinness World Records, the tallest man ever stood eight feet eleven inches tall! Robert Wadlow was born in Alton, Illinois, on February 22, 1918. He died at only twenty-two years old. Reports say he was able to carry his father up the stairs of the family home at age nine! He wore size 37AA shoes, had hands more than a foot long, and an arm span of nearly nine and a half feet.

QUESTION 2

I don't like things about my body — will they get better?

This question is one of the ones I get asked most when I have the opportunity to sit and talk with young men about all the changes they are experiencing. And if there is one thing I can guarantee you, even more changes are coming!

Most boys become very, very self-conscious about their physical development during puberty. But these changes can cause embarrassment if your friends or parents—or even worse, girls or bullies—comment on them.

Throughout our discussions, I want you to learn about these changes. But first, let me address your comment about not liking your body. Remember, you were created by God. I have some thoughts for you to consider.

The Bible says God designed you. It claims that God formed

you—he knit you together—while you were still in your mother's womb.

> For you created my inmost being; you knit me together in my mother's womb. I praise you because I am fearfully and wonderfully made; your works are wonderful, I know that full well. My frame was not hidden from you when I was made in the secret place. When I was woven together in the depths of the earth. Your eyes saw my unformed body; all the days ordained for me were written in your book before one of them came to be. *Psalm 139:13–16*

In other words, God planned and developed you—he is your personal architect, and he caused your body to form and grow. He wove you together like a weaver might create a piece of art with yarn or string.

You are *wonderfully made*, which means you are distinguished—a wonder. Your Creator has designed you so that you are completely unique—one of a kind.

> For we are God's handiwork, created in Christ Jesus to do good works, which God prepared in advance for us to do.
> *Ephesians 2:10*

The Greek word for *handiwork, or workmanship,* is *poiema* (poy'-ay-mah), which means *that which is made personally by the Creator.* It is the origin of the English word *poem.* This Bible verse is an amazing pronouncement—God the Creator personally made *you*!

No one else in the past or in the future will have your fingerprints, or your DNA pattern, or the pattern of the veins on the back of your hand, or your exact personality.

Not only does God have a blueprint for your body, but he has also designed a special life plan just for you. Here are just a few verses describing this:

Many are the plans in a person's heart, but it is the Lord's purpose that prevails. *Proverbs 19:21*

Therefore, my dear friends, as you have always obeyed—not only in my presence, but now much more in my absence—continue to work out your salvation with fear and trembling, for it is God who works in you to will and to act in order to fulfill his good purpose. *Philippians 2:12–13*

And we know that in all things God works for the good of those who love him, who have been called according to his purpose. For those God foreknew he also predestined to be conformed to the image of his Son.... *Romans 8:28–29*

When Jesus came to Earth, he compared his purpose and plan for you with that of your enemy, the Devil:

The thief comes only to steal and kill and destroy; I have come that [you] may have life, and have it to the full.

John 10:10

This means God's plan for you includes his using what you or others may see as imperfections. What may appear from our human perspective to be a design flaw can be used by God for the benefit of any young man that trusts his creator.

God knows you. He loves you. He created you. He designed you. Through your God-given faith, you can grow in your understanding of God's plan for you. This will allow you to increase your willingness to trust and obey him and to thank him for the way he made you.

You may say, "Well, it's not fair that _____." (Fill in the blank with the words "I have zits," or "I'm too short," or "My nose is too long," or any other complaints.)

But if you dwell on that, aren't you really saying, "God, I don't trust your design for me! I think I know what's better for me than you do!"

Really?

Imagine you are God. You are perfect and holy and just and loving. You created the universe. You shaped and named all of the solar systems, nebulae, stars, and planets. You formed earth and put all of the plants and animals on it.

Then you make a little boy who begins to grow into a young man. You know why you have put him together the way you have done it. You know that you allowed each thing that the boy sees as a flaw for a specific purpose. You know what is best for him, and you already know the end of his story—you know how everything on his journey through life is going to turn out. You know where he will go to school, what profession he'll choose, who he'll marry, and what he'll accomplish. You love the little boy more than he will ever love himself.

And, most importantly, you know at the end of his life that he will be able to look back and see that your design and plan for him was perfect.

You are planning an incredible eternity for him to spend with you in heaven. In fact, you are planning and building an eternal home for him—so that you and he can be together forever.

Then imagine that little boy looking in the mirror, frowning in disgust, and turning red-faced in anger and pointing a finger at you and screaming, "I can't believe you made me this way. This is *not* fair. Don't you love me? Don't you want the best for me?"

If you were God, how would you feel? I suspect you'd still love that little boy with all your heart. But you'd want to reach out and pull him into your lap—to hug and to hold him, to wipe the tears from his face—and to say, "Hang in there. Just trust in me. We're in this together. I'll be with you always—always. I don't make no junk!" (Though I think God's grammar would probably be better than this.)

Part of becoming a faithful young man who is a follower of Jesus is trusting that God loves you, that he is in control, that what you are experiencing does not surprise him, and that if you love him and are called to his purpose, then all things will work out for good and to glorify him. It's placing your faith in the fact that his ways are better than your ways.

From my perspective, it's perfectly okay to wonder, "God, what are you doing? What's your plan here? What are you trying to teach me?" It's even honest and truthful to admit to him that you aren't comfortable with certain things he is doing.

But it's wise to understand that God is God and you are not. As the Lord himself told Isaiah:

> "For my thoughts are not your thoughts, neither are your ways my ways," declares the Lord. "As the heavens are higher than the earth, so are my ways higher than your ways and my thoughts than your thoughts." *Isaiah 55:8–9*

The apostle Paul said it this way:

> Oh, the depth of the riches of the wisdom and knowledge of God! How unsearchable his judgments, and his paths beyond tracing out! "Who has known the mind of the Lord? Or who has been his counselor?" *Romans 11:33–34*

A real man, a faithful and true man of God, is one who learns to trust and obey his Creator in the midst of all of the worries and concerns and anxieties of life, accepting God's design of and for him.

So, with that foundation, let's talk about some of the common emotions and questions that most young men feel about the transition from being a boy to becoming a man.

> You know me inside and out, you know every bone in my body; you know exactly how I was made, bit by bit, how I was sculpted from nothing into something. Like an open book, you watched me grow from conception to birth; all the stages of my life were spread out before you, the days of my life all prepared before I'd even lived one day. *Psalm 139:15–16 MSG*

Hot-Cross Bonds

When pastor and author Louie Giglio looks at creation — from distant galaxies to the intricate human cell — he can't help but see God. That's because God's fingerprints are on everything. God even holds our bodies together with a symbol of his never-failing love. In one of his most famous messages, "How Great Is Our God!" Louie talks about a substance called laminin. (More than four million people have viewed this message on You-Tube!)

Laminin is part of a family of proteins that holds our cells together. Think of it as body glue. Scientists who study the human cell under incredibly powerful electron microscopes have found that all laminins investigated so far are in a crosslike shape.

"How crazy is that," Louie says. "The stuff that holds our bodies together, that's holding the linings of your organs together, that's holding your skin on, is in the perfect shape of the cross of our Lord Jesus Christ."

When the Bible says God knits our bodies together, he does it with an amazing cross-shaped molecule. Just think about that! When Louie thinks about it, he can't help but remember what Paul wrote in Colossians 1:16 – 17:

> For in him all things were created: things in heaven and on earth, visible and invisible, whether thrones or powers or rulers or authorities; all things have been created through him and for him. He is before all things, and in him all things hold together.

God's design, love, and power are truly on display in all of creation — even in places that the human eye cannot see. Don't you just love laminin?

QUESTION 3

Why isn't my body changing like I expected?

I remember having this question when I was a boy. It seemed like I was developing more slowly than *any* of my friends. My facial hair came in later. My growth spurt began later. In the ninth grade, I was a ninety-eight-pound weakling.

In all my years as a family physician, one of the things that seems to bother my young patients the most is a delay in maturity. When your development is behind those in your school or neighborhood, it can cause you to wonder if you are normal, or if you are being punished for something.

What I did not know then was that I was totally normal. So whether you are maturing more slowly or faster than your friends—or running right in the middle of the pack—likely you're on target for your divine design.

Nevertheless, those of us who are on the slower end of things when it comes to our physical development tend to spend a lot of time worrying about when our bodies will develop. We wonder when our voices will get deeper, when we'll begin to shave, or when we'll get hair under our arms.

And if your development is behind your friends and other guys in your class, like mine was, this can become even more painfully obvious when you shower with others after a gym class or a sports event.

The fact is that it is completely normal for physical development to start at different times and move along at different rates for each person. Once the first changes begin, it usually takes several years before all the changes of puberty are complete—and on top of this, there's a ton of variation from boy to boy.

So during the teenage years, two normal-developing guys who are the same age can appear quite different from one another. One can look older and more physically mature, but the one who started slower *will* catch up in time.

Although your changes will be different from most of your friends, it will not be terrifically different from your dad! So talking to your dad about when and how he developed may give you an idea of what's ahead for you.

It's important to know that these days, most young boys are growing and developing a tad faster than their dads did. Boys in your generation are growing taller (about one inch taller—on average) and weighing more (about ten pounds—on average) than their fathers.

You are also more likely to go through puberty at a younger age than your dad (about nine months earlier—on average).

So how will *your* body be changing physically and sexually during puberty? Here's a list of when certain changes occur—***on average***:

TEN YEARS: Your male hormones—especially testosterone—are just beginning to become really active, yet there are very few visible signs. Nevertheless, your body is preparing for a series of very dramatic changes over the next few years.

ELEVEN YEARS, SIX MONTHS: Your scrotum is beginning to enlarge, but your penis hasn't begun to change yet. (More in Question 21.)

TWELVE YEARS: You may experience a painful swelling in one or both breasts. This happens to about one in three boys. Don't worry, it's only temporary. (More in Question 17.)

TWELVE YEARS, SIX MONTHS: You begin to grow taller— fast! Your chest wall begins to grow wider and deeper. Fine, soft pubic hair begins to show up just above your penis. The number of erections (the penis getting hard) you have increases. (More in Question 22.)

THIRTEEN YEARS, SIX MONTHS: Your voice begins to deepen and may even crack or squeak when you sing or speak. Your pubic hair begins to darken and become thicker and longer. Your scrotum and testicles are growing more rapidly. The skin on your penis can begin to get darker. Also, your penis begins to grow longer, but does not yet grow bigger around.

FOURTEEN YEARS: Your pubic hair continues to thicken and covers a larger area. Your penis continues to grow— both in length and in width.

FOURTEEN YEARS, SIX MONTHS: Your growth speeds up. Doctors call this a "growth spurt." (More on this in Question 6.) Hair growth begins in your armpits. Your sweat glands begin to produce more sweat, and it begins to develop a distinctive odor (called *body odor* or *BO*). (More in Question 5.) Pimples can begin to form on your face. (More in Question 11.) Your face and body start looking more and more like a young adult.

FIFTEEN YEARS: Facial hair begins to grow on your chin and upper lip. (More in Question 12.) Your skin can get oilier, and your acne can worsen. Your voice gets deeper, and you begin to sound more like a grown man.

SIXTEEN YEARS: Your pubic hair growth and distribution as well as your penis size is similar to a grown man's. Your facial hair is thicker and begins to spread across more of your face. Many young men begin shaving at about this age. Hair growth on your legs begins to increase. You are nearing your full adult height.

EIGHTEEN YEARS: Your body shape is mature.

Let me again emphasize that this is an example of *average* development. At any developmental point on this chart, there is quite a wide range of ages. Also, the order of events can change from one boy to another. There is no right or wrong when it comes to the speed, order, and extent of physical changes during puberty.

Some boys will have hair growing under their arms at the same time their leg hair is beginning to grow and thicken. Other boys could grow hair much later or much earlier than the ages given.

Let me give you a warning: There are many companies that want you to spend money on products they claim will make your body develop faster. But the only things guaranteed to get bigger are their bank accounts as they take your money for products that will not help.

You can't do anything to make your body develop faster than God designed. Of course, you should eat a nutritious diet, exercise, and get enough sleep. But special diets, food supplements, herbs, vitamins, or creams won't do anything to make normal puberty start sooner or happen more quickly.

However, you should know that there are some unhealthy things that can interfere with your development. For example, anabolic steroids (like those used for bodybuilding, which I'll tell you more about in Question 8) can actually cause your testicles to shrink and can damage your liver. They also cause psychological abnormalities, and, believe it or not, make your heart and blood vessels begin to age prematurely.

A number of medical conditions can also delay puberty and development. If you're more than fifteen years old and haven't shown any signs of puberty, be sure to talk with your parents about the possibility of visiting your physician for an evaluation.

Most of the time everything is just fine, but the doctor can determine if there's a problem. There are almost always treatments available that will help you develop—but only under the direction of your physician.

So use the chart above as a general guide only. You can be sure that each of these steps will happen in the timing that God has designed into your system.

> "For I know the plans I have for you," declares the LORD, "plans to prosper you and not to harm you, plans to give you hope and a future." *Jeremiah 29:11*

The Voice

Researchers love to study the male voice. In fact, the male adolescent voice is researched much more frequently than the female changing voice. That's because guys are a lot more interesting. Just kidding! The truth is a young man's voice changes much more drastically than a girl's voice.

At eleven or twelve, most boys could sing in the soprano section of a choir. As a young man grows and his voice changes, it deepens to more of a tenor, baritone, or bass sound. The bass is the lowest of the male vocal types.

When you go through puberty, you probably won't have a deep bass voice. Your voice may even squeak or crack every once in a while. This is caused when your voice box (also called the larynx) and vocal chords grow larger. In some guys, the voice box grows so large it begins to stick out at the front of the neck, causing a lump. This lump is called the Adam's apple. A girl's voice box doesn't grow much during puberty, which is why women don't have Adam's apples.

With a larger voice box (just like with larger feet), it takes some time to adjust and learn control. So as you trip over your feet (see the next question), you may also trip over your voice as it cracks or squeaks. But don't worry, just as you grow more coordinated with your body, you'll adjust and learn to control your new voice too.

QUESTION 4

Why are my feet so big?

When you go through puberty, your body begins a growth spurt. (More on this in Question 6.) Interestingly, not every part of the body grows at the same rate.

It's not at all uncommon for a boy's feet to grow more quickly than the rest of his body. The bad news is you may need new shoes every few months! The good news is this indicates that you have likely entered your adolescent growth spurt.

During your growth spurt, not only your feet, but also your extremities (arms, hands, and legs) and your facial bones will get larger *before* the rest of your body. This is why boys entering their growth spurt often appear to have hands and feet that are out of proportion to the rest of their bodies, and why their faces may appear to be "long."

But you can relax, for three very good reasons: (1) You are much more aware of these changes than those around you. (2) Your trunk, or torso, will begin its growth and then your body will even out. (3) This is all part of God's perfect design for you to transition from being a boy into being a man.

Another common worry during this stage of puberty is clumsiness, which can be very embarrassing. Here's why this happens: When you grow slowly, your brain has time to adjust and learn. God created your brain to know where your hands and legs are at all times—even if your eyes can't see them.

Don't believe it? Just close your eyes and move your fingers, hands, or feet. Your mind's eye knows exactly where they are. Your brain works this way so it can very skillfully help guide your fingers and toes, your hands and your feet, your arms and your legs.

However, when you grow very quickly, it can take your brain a little time to adapt with your growth. Therefore, while your brain is learning and catching up, you may be a bit clumsier than usual.

But don't worry. Although this phase can be awkward and embarrassing, it will pass before you know it.

In the meantime, you can speed up your brain's learning by working out. Exercise—including weight lifting and playing games that seem less clumsy to you—is an effective way to accelerate your brain's learning and reduce clumsiness more quickly. Interactive Metronome is a great PC game that helps improve balance and coordination, as well as Dance Dance Revolution, Wii, or Xbox Kinect video games.

Instead of looking down at your feet or worrying about your clumsiness during this time, look up to God. Ask him what he's up to with you. Use this critical time in your life to take your focus off of *yourself* and focus on *him* more and more!

Even youths grow tired and weary, and young men stumble and fall; but those who hope in the LORD will renew their strength. They will soar on wings like eagles; they will run and not grow weary, they will walk and not be faint.

Isaiah 40:30–31

The Lord makes firm the steps of the one who delights in him; though he may stumble, he will not fall, for the Lord upholds him with his hand.

Psalm 37:23–24

Build Your Brain

Your brain is one of the most powerful super-computers on the planet. By practicing an action over and over, your brain can have your body do it perfectly. If you're feeling clumsy and want to get more coordinated, try these exercises:

- Balance on one leg while moving your other leg out to the side, in front, or behind you.
- Pat your head with one hand, while rubbing your belly in a circular motion with the other.
- Jump in place and try to spin a perfect 180 or 360 degrees.
- Stand with your feet shoulder-width apart. Lift your right knee up as you crossover your left hand and touch the outside of your right knee. Repeat by lifting your left knee and crossing over your right hand to touch it. Continue "marching" in place and touching your knee with the opposite hand.
- Run in a figure eight. Then do it backward!

- Jump rope backward.
- Lay on your belly, then jump to your feet and run ten yards. Gently drop to one knee, then stand up and run another ten yards.
- Gather four objects (balls, cones, etc.). Set one object fifteen feet in front of you, one fifteen feet behind you, and one fifteen feet to each side of you. Stand in the center. Begin by running to the object to your left. Touch it and run to the one all the way to your right. Return to the middle, then run to the object in front of you. Backpedal to the object behind you and then run back to the middle. Once you've mastered this, change up your pattern.

A little bit of exercise and doing these drills every day can help you feel a lot less awkward as your body changes and grows.

QUESTION 5

I've got BO — what's a guy to do?

Most boys will notice, as they begin puberty, that they have new smells coming from under their arms and elsewhere on their bodies — including their feet. That smell is called *body odor* or *BO*, and every boy battles against it. It's not only normal, it's God-designed.

As you enter puberty, hormones activate glands in your skin, and their chemicals begin interacting with the normal bacteria on your body — and that's what causes the new odors. It's basically a chain reaction of stink. One of my professors once told me, "These chemicals put the scent in adole*scent*!" So what can you do to reduce the odor?

Keeping clean by washing with soap is a good way to lessen the smell. If there are fewer skin bacteria to interact with the oily secretions of your skin, it equals less body odor. You might want to take a shower every day, either in the morning before school, or at night. But if the rest of your skin gets too dry or scaly, you could just use soap to wash your armpits and groin, because that's where the glands are located that make the odor.

And it's a good idea to use deodorant or an antiperspirant every day too. (The basic difference between deodorants and antiperspirants is that the former cuts down on what makes you stink when you do sweat, while the latter keeps you from sweating.) You can find products that combine an antiperspirant and a deodorant in a spray or stick. I always tell young men to "stick with the stick," because it's easier to use.

By the way, don't forget that foot odor can invade your shoes. To help prevent this, you can use foot powder in your shoes or on your feet before you put on socks and wash your athletic shoes every month—if they're not leather. Also consider always wearing cotton socks or shoes that breathe (like canvas shoes or sandals when allowed).

When you notice you have some BO, remember to (1) wash up, (2) deodorize, and (3) thank the Lord that you're becoming a man. But most importantly, use your smell as a reminder to ask yourself whether your life is the fragrant aroma to others that God wants it to be.

> But thanks be to God, who ... uses us to spread the aroma
> of the knowledge of him everywhere. For we are to God the
> pleasing aroma of Christ among those who are being saved
> and those who are perishing.   *2 Corinthians 2:14–15*

Smell of Success

Experts estimate that twelve billion dollars are spent every year on perfume and cologne by people living in the United States and Europe. Obviously, smelling good is important to a lot of people. And it should be important to you too.

When you smell good, you attract people. Businesses have found that smells can be very important too.

Have you ever noticed that grocery stores often smell like fresh-baked bread, even when there's no fresh-baked bread to be bought? That's because the smell of fresh-baked bread makes people hungry and causes them to buy more food.

Don't believe it? Well, a pizza store in France did a three-week experiment. The first week they didn't add any smell. During the second week, the owner used a diffuser to pump out the slight scent of lemons. In the third week, lavender was added to the air. The result? People bought more and spent more time in the store during the second and third weeks. Sales soared twenty percent in the third week!

So remember, even if smells don't matter much to you, they make a big difference for the people around you.

QUESTION 6

What's a growth spurt?

During puberty, if you notice your shirt-sleeves are getting shorter or your pants seem hiked up (as in, they look ready for a flood, hence the term "floods"), that's because you're experiencing a major growth spurt.

Spurt is a word used to describe a short burst of activity, or something that happens in a hurry. So a *growth spurt* is just that: your body is growing, and it's happening really fast!

A growth spurt is caused by the combined effect of testosterone and growth hormone. Your growth spurt during puberty will be the last time your body will grow significantly taller. Toward the end of your growth spurt, the growth plates of your bones will fuse so that they will not grow longer. When this happens, viola, you have reached your adult height!

Although the typical guy is usually about one inch shorter than the typical girl before puberty, men are, on average, more than five inches taller than women. The reason for this is that although guys generally start growth spurts later than girls, our growth spurts last a lot longer—so we catch up and eventually pass them.

In fact, when the growth spurt is at its peak, some guys grow four or more inches in a single year!

Occasionally, I'll see a guy whose growth is lagging behind significantly. This is called *constitutional growth delay* and can result in a boy being a slow grower or a *late bloomer*.

When I see this, I order X-rays of the boy's bones and compare them with X-rays of what's considered average for that age. Teens with constitutional growth delay tend to have bones that look younger than what is expected for their age.

The good news is that almost all of these teens will have a growth spurt, although a bit delayed, and continue growing and developing into manhood. They almost always catch up with their peers by the time they're young adults.

Now let's move on to answer some of your questions about other aspects of puberty.

> Jabez cried out to the God of Israel, "Oh, that you would bless me and enlarge my territory! Let your hand be with me, and keep me from harm" ... And God granted his request.
>
> *1 Chronicles 4:10*

Late Basketball Bloomer

David Robinson will always be known as one of the best basketball players to ever play the game. During his fourteen-year NBA career, he scored more than 20,000 points, grabbed over 10,000 rebounds, blocked nearly 3,000 shots, and earned countless honors. He helped the San Antonio Spurs win two world championships and was the league's most valuable player and defensive player of the year. He was even named to the list of the fifty greatest players in NBA history.

Maybe you knew all of that. But did you know David entered high school as a five-feet-nine-inch freshman? He ended high school six feet, seven inches tall. He only played basketball one year, because he preferred gymnastics.

David enrolled at the Naval Academy but didn't play much as a freshman. Then he grew another five inches between his freshman and sophomore years of college, ending up at seven feet, one inch. It was at that point that David thought maybe God planned for him to have a future in basketball. He was right!

QUESTION 7

I keep eating, so why am I still too little?

A young man recently contacted me with a similar concern. He wrote: "I want to try out for the football team, but the coach says I'm not the correct weight. I'm trying to bulk up but am still too small. Is there something wrong with me?"

My answer: Chances are there's nothing wrong at all, but here's how you can find out.

(A) You need to record an accurate height and weight for yourself. You can get tips on doing this in Appendix A.

(B) You need the height of your biological mother and father. If you cannot get the actual measurements, an estimate will work.

(C) You need to go online to use some Internet-based tools.

Step 1: See if your height is normal for your age by using a *stature-for-age chart*. I have the Centers for Disease Control (CDC) chart in Appendix B.

You will notice on these charts that there is a tremendous variation for normal. For example, at twelve years of age, the *normal* young man can be anywhere from fifty-three and one half inches (about four-and-a-half feet tall) to sixty-four and one half inches tall (about five-and-a-third feet tall). That's nearly a foot (as in twelve-inches) difference!

If your height is abnormally high or low, then your doctor should evaluate you. However, if your height is in the normal range, then the real question is not how tall you are now, but how tall you will likely be after puberty.

It's important to understand that to a great extent your height is determined by the adult height of your biological parents. You can use a couple of Internet tools to help you predict where you might end up.

The first tool is one in which you enter your biological mom's and your biological dad's adult heights to get a guesstimate of your height when you are fully grown. That tool can be found at www.keepkidshealthy.com/welcome/htcalculator.html.

The second tool, which is a bit more accurate, can be found at http://children.webmd.com/healthtool-kids-height-predictor.

Step 2: See if your weight is normal for your age and height by using a body mass index (BMI) percentile calculator (Appendix C). This calculator will tell your BMI percentile. Here's how to interpret the number:

- Less than the fifth percentile, you are underweight.
- Fifth percentile to less than the seventy-fifth percentile, you are at a healthy weight.
- Seventy-fifth percentile to less than the eighty-fifth percentile, you are at a normal weight, but you are potentially "at risk" to become overweight.

- Eighty-fifth to less than the ninety-fifth percentile, you are overweight and at risk for becoming obese — if this is your percentile, be sure to read Question 9.
- Ninety-fifth percentile or greater, you are obese — and if this is the case, absolutely be sure to study Question 9.

Now, if you are underweight, overweight, or obese, you should see your doctor. If you're overweight or obese, you and your parents can read much more about how to deal with this in my book *SuperSized Kids*: *How to Rescue Your Child from the Obesity Threat* or on my www.SuperSizedKids.com website.

However, if you're between the fifth and eighty-fifth percentiles, you're considered normal. Once again, notice the tremendous variation for normal. For example, at twelve, a *normal* young man can weigh anywhere from 66 to 128 pounds — that's a range of over sixty pounds! And if you are in the fifth to seventy-fifth percentile range, you can safely put on weight. If you are above the seventy-fifth percentile and want to put on some muscle weight, get some advice from a physician, coach, or trainer.

To safely put on weight, there are a couple of strategies I recommend to my young patients:

Strategy No. 1: Build muscle with strength training

Don't confuse strength training with weightlifting, bodybuilding, or power-lifting. These can put too much strain on young muscles, tendons, and areas of cartilage that haven't yet turned to bone (called *growth plates*) — especially when proper technique is sacrificed in favor of lifting larger amounts of weight.

But there are tremendous potential benefits with strength training that is done properly. And strength training isn't just for athletes. Strength training can include these benefits:

- Increased muscle strength and endurance
- Protection of muscles and joints from injury

- Stronger bones
- Healthy blood pressure and cholesterol levels
- Boosted metabolism
- Maintenance of a healthy weight

You can do many strength-training exercises with your own body weight by using inexpensive resistance tubing. Free weights and machine weights are other options.

Children under eight years old should not begin strength training. Prior to then, kids can improve their muscle strength through active play. But as early as eight years old, strength training can become a valuable part of an overall fitness plan — as long as you practice proper technique and form. And remember that "bulking up" is most safely reserved until after puberty.

Strength-Training 101

- Get coached. Many health clubs like the YMCA offer strength-training classes especially for young men. You may also want to look for a personal trainer who offers youth training. The coach or trainer can create a safe, effective program based on your age, size, skills, and sports interests.
- Warm up and cool down. Warming up before working out is extremely important. To avoid injuries, personal trainers insist on at least five minutes of stretching and aerobic activity like jogging in place or jumping rope. Stretching afterward also reduces injury and sore muscles.
- Accept supervision. A parent, coach, or other adult is an important part of youth strength training. Don't do it alone.

- Keep it light. Boys can safely lift adult-sized weights, as long as the weight is light enough. In most cases, one set of twelve to fifteen repetitions is all it takes. Resistance tubing and body-weight exercises, such as push-ups, are equally effective.
- Use proper technique. Rather than focusing on the amount of weight you lift, stress proper form during each exercise. This is where a coach or trainer really helps. Gradually increase the resistance, weight, or the number of repetitions as you get stronger and older.
- Rest between workouts. Make sure you rest at least one full day between exercising each specific muscle group. Two or three strength-training sessions a week are plenty.
- Keep it fun.

Remember that results won't come overnight, but with consistency, you will notice a difference in muscle strength and endurance in about three weeks. Plus you've established a healthy routine that will last a lifetime.

Strategy 2: Eat more healthy calories

More food does not equal healthy calories. Read labels. Look for nutritional content. Foods that have little to no vitamins or minerals are known as empty calories. These foods give you calories, but no nutrition. For example, eating an entire bag of chips is more likely to make your face break out than gain a pound. Eating foods high in protein and healthy fats will help your body and your health. Some ideas include dried fruit and nuts, bananas, avocados, cheese and crackers, string cheese, peanut butter and crackers.

> ## Follow this formula: 5 – 2 – 1 – 0
>
> • Five: Eat five servings of fruits and vegetables every day.
> • Two: Two-hour screen time limit (Internet, TV, video games, phone).
> • One: Exercise one hour every day.
> • Zero: Consume zero sweetened beverages daily.

Healthy Calorie Ideas

- Starchy carbohydrates. Adding starchy carbohydrates, such as pasta, rice, and potatoes, along with strength training, can help you gain healthy weight. Other foods with high carbohydrate content include French toast, pancakes, bread, and hot cereal.
- Dairy products. Adding cheese, cottage cheese, yogurt, and even ice cream may help with weight gain — but stick with fat-free milk.
- Mega-Milkshakes: Along with milk and ice cream, protein or breakfast powder can add 400 healthy calories to your diet, as well as fresh or frozen fruit, especially bananas, and pudding or peanut butter.
- The power of peanut butter: One tablespoon packs healthy protein and 100 calories.
- Snack pack: Add two or three high-calorie, healthy snacks to your daily diet.

The bottom line is that you can increase your weight and strength as you grow through adolescence — just do so wisely and safely. In the next chapter, I'll give you more ideas on how to build muscle.

> The righteous will flourish like a palm tree, they will grow like a cedar of Lebanon; planted in the house of the Lord, they will flourish in the courts of our God. *Psalm 92:12–13*

For our light and momentary troubles are achieving for us an eternal glory that far outweighs them all. So we fix our eyes not on what is seen, but on what is unseen, since what is seen is temporary, but what is unseen is eternal.

2 Corinthians 4:17–18

We ought always to thank God for you, brothers and sisters, and rightly so, because your faith is growing more and more, and the love all of you have for one another is increasing.   *2 Thessalonians 1:3*

Get Active

How many TV commercials do you watch every year? Take a guess.

The American Academy of Pediatrics (AAP) estimates that the average American kid sees 40,000 commercials each year. That averages out to nearly 110 commercials every day! And that means a lot of kids are spending a ton of time in front of the TV.

Studies show kids between eight and eighteen years old spend nearly four hours a day in front of a TV screen and another two hours on the computer. That's almost as much as a full-time job. And considering the fact that you're only in school for around nine months a year, it's very possible that kids spend more time in front of a screen than they do in a classroom!

If you want to live a healthy life and build a strong body, one of the best things you can do is get away from the TV and computer. You don't have to join a sports team. Just walking the dog, helping with yard work, riding your bike, or playing outside with friends can make you fit and strong.

Fight against the trend of more and more kids being stuck inside playing video games or watching TV. Get active and get outside. Your body will thank you for it.

QUESTION 8

How can I get bigger muscles?

I entered the ninth grade as the proverbial ninety-eight-pound weakling. I remember wanting not only to increase my weight, but also to build up my muscles—especially my chest and arm muscles.

My parents signed me up for a YMCA membership, and I began working out, but it wasn't very long before some of the older guys began talking about pills I could take to build muscle a lot quicker.

The pills weren't cheap—but they sure were tempting. Looking back on that time, I'm glad I couldn't afford them. Why? Because taking pills that are safe do *not* work, and those that work are *not* safe. Let me explain.

Warning 1: Don't depend upon medications, natural or not.

In my book *Alternative Medicine: The Christian Handbook*, I take an evidence-based look at natural medications (herbs, vitamins, and supplements). Many of them are safe and effective. However, when it comes to this topic, the bottom line is that supplements, vitamins, and protein drinks will do almost nothing to speed the process of growing muscle or height. In other words, although they are safe, they do *not* work.

I'm most commonly asked about the supplement creatine, which is a commonly used sports supplement that has become very popular with weight lifters and football players. Basically, for recreational athletes and those who exercise aerobically, creatine has virtually no benefit. Also, we don't know if it's safe for younger athletes. For these reasons, the American College of Sports Medicine recommends against creatine supplementation for those under eighteen years of age.

If you feel you must take a supplement, choose a multivitamin. It contains the nutrients that should be in a healthy diet and is not likely to cause you harm.

Warning 2: Don't try anabolic steroids.

First of all, there's a massive difference between anabolic, or bodybuilding steroids, and the steroids your family doctor may prescribe for allergies or asthma.

Anabolic steroids are prescription drugs, but they are easily available illegally on the Internet and at gyms and clubs. These products are so potentially dangerous to you that in some states there's a law that a warning must be posted on the walls of locker rooms:

Warning: Improper use of anabolic steroids may cause serious or fatal health problems, such as heart disease, stroke, cancer, growth deformities, infertility, personality changes, severe acne, and baldness. Possession, sale, or use of anabolic steroids without a valid prescription is a crime punishable by a fine and imprisonment.

Do these steroids work? Absolutely. Taking these substances

while working out can increase your muscle mass 10 to 15 percent. But the risk is huge. In other words, they work, but they are *not* safe.

Besides the risks listed above, other risks include the shrinkage of your testicles, infertility, breast enlargement, short stature (it may stop your height growth), and bad effects on your blood lipid levels (like your cholesterol).

But other side affects concern me even more. These steroids can increase your risk of heart attack and stroke later in life. If you choose to use, you may be reducing the quality and the quantity of your life.

Anabolic steroids can actually change your personality or lead to crazy (psychotic) outbursts of anger or other uncontrollable behavior. And because many of these substances are made illegally, they could be contaminated with other unknown ingredients.

Warning 3: Be very careful how you work out.

Many young athletes ask me about resistance training with elastic bands or elastic tubing versus using free weights. I find that many people (your dad may be one) are skeptical that working out with elastic bands could be effective when compared to "good old-fashioned" free weights.

However, many young teens have ruined arm muscles from pumping weights that are more than they could handle.

However, as one coach reviewing this book told me, "Having coached baseball for many years, parents and coaches all too often have their young teens pumping weights, maxing out their limits. I have seen too many arms ruined because their muscles were not able to deal with the stress. I always taught the use of bands and resistance."

So what's better—resistance bands or weights? First, let me define each.

Resistance bands are lightweight elastic strips or tubes that come in a variety of colors. With most systems, each color represents a different level of resistance. These bands can be used alone or with special accessories, such as door attachments or handles, to give you a wide variety of exercises to choose from.

Free weights are basically any kind of weight that is not attached to a machine. Dumbbells, barbells, weighted medicine balls, and sandbags are all examples of free weights.

Since elastic bands are much lighter than heavy free weights, some people mistakenly believe they are less effective at building strength and muscle. In actuality, researchers have shown that *peak load* (the amount of force needed to activate and build muscle fibers) is the same with elastic resistance devices as it is with free weights.

Elastic bands and free weights similarities:

- Both build muscle strength,
- Increase muscle mass,
- Eliminate body fat,
- Provide resistance that builds muscle strength,
- Permit a free range of motion (unrestricted movement in any direction),
- Allow for movement at variable speeds (perform exercises faster or slower), and
- Enable progressive resistance (so that you can increase or decrease resistance).

However, there are a number of differences that lead me to recommend elastic-band training for younger men instead of free weights. The most significant is an increased risk of injury with free weights.

One of the biggest differences between free weights and elastic resistance systems is that free weights rely on gravity in order to provide the resistance they offer. By using gravity for resistance, the weight builds momentum with each exercise and increases the chance of your losing control during exercise and injuring yourself.

Another elastic-band bonus is that they actually allow you to exercise using a wider variety of natural body movements like you would in your everyday life or in your specific sport. For example, with a band you can make a punching motion that mimics the way your arm would move when you throw a baseball or jab a punching bag. If you made the same motion while holding a dumbbell, the weight could put more strain on your shoulder joint or overextend your elbow. Bands allow you to utilize movements that you cannot with free weights, such as twisting and turning from side to side, or doing punches and sidekicks.

Resistance bands also minimize the amount of "cheating" that can be done. With free weights, it's much easier to use other muscles to help those you want to work out, while bands isolate the muscle or muscle group being exercised.

Plus, elastic bands are compact, light, portable, and less expensive. Beside convenience, because they offer smoother exercise with less injury, I'm finding that resistance-band exercises are quickly replacing traditional free weights.

To sum up, if your physical design hinders you from being successful in a particular sport, then begin to ask God what he has designed you for. What does he want *you* to do? What plans does he have for *you*? What skills and desires and hopes has he given you?

If you hope to be an athlete, but God has not given you the body or the skills to do that, then likely that is *not* his plan for you.

However, if you are concerned about whether your growth and development are normal or not, be sure to talk to your parents. They may want you to see your doctor just to be sure everything is okay.

> And we pray this in order that you may live a life worthy of the Lord and please him in every way: bearing fruit in every good work, growing in the knowledge of God, being strengthened with all power according to his glorious might so that you may have great endurance and patience, and giving joyful thanks to the Father, who has qualified you to share in the inheritance of his holy people in the kingdom of light.　　　　　*Colossians 1:10 – 12*

> Only God ... makes things grow.
>
> 　　　　　*1 Corinthians 3:7*

Stay Off the Juice

The good news is studies show steroid use among teenagers is declining. The bad news is between three and six percent of students in the United States have tried them. That means hundreds of thousands of young men and women are at risk of suffering the damaging side effects of these illegal drugs, which can also be called juice, gym candy, pumpers, or stackers.

Steroids aren't new. Weight lifters have used them for years. One of the first football players to admit steroid use was Lyle Alzado, who terrorized backfields as a defensive lineman in the 1970s and 80s. Lyle said he first started using steroids in college and become so addicted to them that he continued taking them for more than fifteen years — often costing him more than $30,000 a year. Lyle died at age forty-three of cancer. Although doctors couldn't confirm a link, Lyle blamed his cancer on his steroid use.

It cost him much more. Lyle's aggressiveness on the field often spilled out in his regular life. Steroids mess with a person's emotions. Some link steroid use to depression and suicide. And steroids are known to create horrible acne. Some steroid users report grotesque and lifelong scars on their chest and body due to explosive steroid acne.

So if you're ever tempted to build muscle using the shortcut of steroids, think about all the nasty side effects. And stay off the juice!

QUESTION 9

I'm overweight. How much is too much?

Fact: Most overweight and obese young men will *not* outgrow it. In fact, 70 to 80 percent of obese adolescents will remain so as adults.

But there's more bad news. If you're obese as a young man, you have an increased risk of heart disease as early as twenty-five years of age. This risk is much higher for obese boys than girls.

Worse yet, if you're obese, you're also more likely to die in early adulthood. Obesity can actually reduce your life expectancy by somewhere between eight and twenty years!

I'm not telling you this to scare you, but to inform you of the medical statistics. In every chapter of this book, I want to give you all the facts. However, the bad news is balanced by some very good news. You can improve your health today and in the future by making wise decisions about your nutrition, activity, and sleep.

If you're overweight but not yet obese, you can prevent yourself from becoming obese by making healthy choices. Even if your weight is normal, use this information to develop and maintain a permanent healthy lifestyle.

The hard facts on poor choices:

1. Poor nutrition choices: Eating too many foods high in "bad" sugar and fats, including sweets, processed, junk, and fast foods.
2. Poor activity choices: Too much screen time and not enough active play and exercise.
3. Poor sleep choices: Staying up too late, and getting less than nine or ten hours of sleep every night (more on this in the next chapter).

The hard results:

1. Obesity
2. High blood pressure
3. Heart disease
4. Heart attack
5. Diabetes
6. Arthritis
7. Stroke
8. Cancer

If you're overweight or obese, your body could already be building up disease that will attack later, even if you're feeling pretty good right now.

The decisions you make now—about diet, activity, exercise, sleep, smoking, drinking alcohol, and drug use—will make a difference for a lifetime. Decide right now to live a healthy lifestyle, commit to making good choices, and you'll live longer and you'll live better.

Medical studies make it very clear that the nutrition and exercise habits you begin in middle school and high school (and college) are the habits you're most likely to continue for life. So choosing now to eat well and exercise is actually an investment in your future!

How'd you do? Now why don't you score your family? Spend ten to fifteen minutes filling out the online interactive quiz I developed especially for parents and children at www.supersized-kids.com/resources/quiz/index.asp. The quiz assesses your family's risk in becoming overweight and ways you can work together to control and dramatically reduce this risk. You'll be graded in three areas, activity, nutrition, and family BMI (body mass index). Completing this questionnaire will give you an instant snapshot of your risk status. If you don't make straight A's, look for changes you and your family can make. The website and my *SuperSized Kids* book will give more ideas.

You could even help lead your family's action plan. Go to www.DrWalt.com and check out the family fitness plan, *SuperSized Kids Eight-Week Plan*. Jot down some ideas you and your family might try together.

Ideas For Healthy Living

1. _____

2. _____

3. _____

4. _____

5. _____

6. _____

7. _____

8. _____

9. _____

Show your list to your parents. Maybe even schedule a family meeting to discuss any problems you found and possible actions you could take as a family. See if your siblings and parents have any other ideas and find out what you'd *all* be willing to try.

Once you have a plan, it's time to get started! It will take some time and effort, but remember, small changes can result in big benefits. The simple steps in the eight-week plan will work! In fact, you can meet other families on the website who have used the plan with success!

Don't give up! At the end of the eight weeks, retake the Super-Sized quiz and see how much you've improved. If you're willing, try another eight-week plan (also on the website).

Think of it like this: If you put a little money in a savings account each week, the interest slowly begins to build, barely noticeable at first, but as time goes on the interest grows faster and faster. Before you know it, small amounts of money become huge sums of cash!

It's the same way with your health. Good habits now make a winning recipe for a long and healthy life. Even if you don't recognize it now, as you get older, you'll be thankful for the choices you made. Now is the time to start taking small, simple steps.

Long life to you! Good health to you and your household!
And good health to all that is yours!   *1 Samuel 25:6*

Do not be wise in your own eyes; fear the Lord and shun evil. This will bring health to your body and nourishment to your bones. *Proverbs 3:7–8*

Though one may be overpowered, two can defend themselves. A cord of three strands is not quickly broken.

Ecclesiastes 4:12

Super Sized

Experts say one out of three kids in the United States is now considered overweight or obese. Some of the problem is lack of exercise. Another part is poor diet.

In 2003, filmmaker Morgan Spurlock combined those two characteristics as he ate only McDonald's food for thirty days, while doing little to no exercise. Not surprisingly, Morgan gained more than twenty-four pounds in a month and saw his cholesterol level jump to an unhealthy 230.

Does that mean that all McDonald's food is bad for you? No. But Morgan's experience proves you have to watch what you eat.

Morgan ate an average of 5,000 calories a day. The recommended calorie intake for a man Morgan's age and weight was 2,300. For every 3,500 calories a person consumes without burning it off through exercise, he will gain one pound. So just by eating as much as he did, Morgan was bound to gain weight. Plus, about one-third of his calories came from sugar. Dietary guidelines say only about 6 percent of your calories should come from sugar. Morgan ate more than five times that amount!

The truth is to a large extent you control how healthy you will be. God has given you an amazing body, and it's your job to feed it right and make sure it gets enough exercise.

QUESTION 10

How much sleep do I need?

If you're the average preteen, it's probably safe to say you are not getting as much sleep as you need. Medical studies show that more and more young people are staying up late and falling asleep at school. Increasingly, more and more children are arriving late at school — having overslept!

If you're seven to twelve years old, you need ten to eleven hours of sleep each day. However, studies show the average kid this age only gets eight to nine hours of sleep. That's not enough.

During your teen years, you need eight to nine hours of sleep each night. But researchers have found that guys this age only get between six and seven hours of sleep.

If you don't get enough sleep, your academic and athletic

performances may begin to drop off dramatically. Guys who lack sleep are more likely to fall asleep in class, have difficulty getting up in the morning, have a reduced ability to concentrate and learn, and may even suffer from depression.

Sleep may also affect your grades. Children who get the least amount of sleep are more likely to get C's and D's. However, children who sleep the most are more likely to get A's and B's.

Not only does sleep help your grades, but it helps keep you healthy. Restful sleep reenergizes you and allows your body and mind to recover and prepare for the next day. Also, restful sleep promotes healthy bone growth, helps form red blood cells that deliver oxygen to your body and brain, and releases a growth hormone that helps tissues grow properly.

Plus, the more sleep you get, the less likely you are to be overweight or obese. And if you're already overweight or obese, increasing your sleep may help you lose weight.

Do's and Don'ts for Healthy Z's

- Avoid caffeine after 4 p.m., such as sodas, energy drinks, coffee, or chocolate. (Yes, chocolate has caffeine!)
- Avoid exciting, violent, or scary shows before bedtime. (Stop watching thirty minutes before bed — sixty would be better.)
- Don't use a computer for the last hour or so before bedtime. The light from the computer sends signals to your brain that it's time to wake up. The same can be true for the TV.
- Avoid books that might keep you from falling asleep.
- Don't nap excessively. Napping more than thirty minutes may keep you from falling asleep later. In fact, a ten to twenty minute "power nap" has been proven to

give you the most energy (compared to longer naps), and it doesn't prevent you from falling asleep at night.

- Don't wait until the night before to study for a big test. Staying up all night can really mess up your sleep patterns and your performance on the test. Plan to do your studying ahead of time.

- Do exercise regularly, but not right before bed. Regular exercise improves sleep. But exercising an hour or two before bedtime makes falling asleep more difficult.

- Do try to go to bed and wake up at the same time every day (or at least most days of the week).

- Do try to stick with your regular sleep schedule on weekends too. You can't catch up on missed sleep from the week before.

- Don't sleep with a pet — especially dogs — as they move around all night and can keep you from deep sleep.

- Do get into bright light in the morning. It will wake you up and get you going.

- Do try to unwind from the day. You can do this by praying, reading your Bible or a peaceful book, journaling, or listening to soothing music.

- Do turn off your cell phone and computer. Keeping these electronics on can stop you from having a good night's sleep.

- Do make sure your room is cool and absolutely as dark as possible.

Getting a good night's sleep will improve your physical, emotional, relational, and spiritual health—as well as your academic and athletic accomplishments.

I lie down and sleep; I wake again, because the Lord sustains me.

Psalm 3:5

In peace I will lie down and sleep, for you alone, Lord, make me dwell in safety.   *Psalm 4:8*

… He (the Lord) grants sleep to those he loves.
                                                Psalm 127:2

When you lie down, you will not be afraid; when you lie down, your sleep will be sweet.   *Proverbs 3:24*

The sleep of a laborer is sweet, whether they eat little or much, but as for the rich, their abundance permits them no sleep.   *Ecclesiastes 5:12*

Everybody Sleeps

Humans aren't the only ones who need sleep. Most animals have a daily pattern of sleep and activity. Take a look at how long these different animals sleep:

- Brown bat — 19.9 hours
- Tiger — 15.8 hours
- Squirrel — 14.9 hours
- Lion — 13.5 hours
- Cat — 12.1 hours
- Dog — 10.6 hours
- Human (adult) — 8 hours
- Goat — 5.3 hours
- Cow — 3.9 hours
- African Elephant — 3.3 hours
- Giraffe — 1.9 hours
- Bottlenose dolphin — 10.4 hours

Dolphins often sleep while swimming by shutting down half of their brain. That means one eye stays open to watch for predators, obstacles, and other animals. Usually after two hours, the dolphin will switch and have the other eye open and other side of the brain rest. Fish sleep with their eyes open all the time, because most don't have eyelids.

QUESTION 11

My acne is scary! What's wrong with my face?

First of all, there's nothing wrong with your face. Acne is a natural part of growing up. And you should know it is not usually caused by eating the wrong foods (like pizza or chocolate) or drinking lots of soda or sugary drinks.

Acne is caused by overactive oil glands in the skin, especially on the face, neck, chest, and back. These oil glands become stimulated with the same hormones that God designed to carry you through puberty. Some young men have more of a reaction to their hormone levels than others, so acne varies from boy to boy. Stress can also make acne worse. But the good news is there are ways reduce the number and severity of breakouts.

Save Face

- Keep your skin clean. It helps remove excess surface oils and dead skin cells that can clog your pores. But washing too much can actually cause damage by over drying your skin or irritating existing acne.
- Use your hands to wash your face and body instead of a washcloth. Never scrub your skin.
- Keep it simple. Wash your face with a moisturizing soap twice a day. Some physicians recommend an antibacterial soap.
- Avoid harsh alcohol-based cleansers or cleansers that contain oil.
- Wash after exercising because sweat and dirt can clog your pores and make your acne worse.
- If you work around greasy food or oil, wash your face and other acne-prone areas as soon as possible.
- Gently pat dry with a clean towel.
- If you can't live without hair gel, be sure to keep it away from your face as much as possible. Many hair products contain chemicals that can make acne worse.
- Try not to pick at your face or lean your chin on your hands.

Over-the-counter acne medications can also help clear up mild acne. Look for a product with the chemical called benzyl peroxide (BP), which works as a peeling agent, increases the turnover of skin cells, and helps clear pores. Sometimes BP can lightly bleach clothing, so it's better to use it at night.

Start with a product that contains 5 percent BP and apply it at night after washing your face. Since BP causes dryness and flaking, it's important to keep your skin hydrated by using moisturizing lotion after the BP. I recommend lotions instead of creams, as they are less likely to clog your pores, and make sure it's fragrance free and "non-comedogenic," which means that it doesn't contribute to acne.

After four-five days of consistent use, if your acne hasn't improved and your skin isn't irritated, try applying the cream twice a day or switching to a cream with 10 percent BP.

If these tips don't work and your acne does not get better (or if it's worsening), then see your doctor. Acne will improve with simple prescription gels or creams, a prescription pill, or on occasion, a combination of both. But you'll need to be patient. It may take a little while to find the exact combination of prescriptions to help clear up your acne. There are many, many options, and one will help, eventually.

Also, don't be embarrassed to talk about your acne with your doctor. He or she is trained to help get your skin to look its best and has probably dealt with it too. The best news of all is that, in general, acne decreases and is usually gone by the time you complete puberty.

But while you're battling acne, you may be *very* tempted to squeeze and pop a big pimple. However, this may actually make your acne worse by forcing the infected material to go deeper into the skin and causing even more swelling and redness. Popping pimples may even leave a purplish mark that stays on the skin for weeks. Sometimes, squeezing pimples can even lead to scarring. *Yikes!*

Acne isn't the only skin problem you have to worry about as you go through puberty. You should also protect yourself against sunburn. If you are going to be in the sun for more than twenty minutes during the hours of 9 a.m. to 4 p.m., protect any exposed skin with a moisturizing lotion containing ultraviolet (sunlight) protection. Look for a lotion with an SPF of at least fifteen.

Note that more sunscreen manufacturers are coming out with products that have an SPF of forty-five, fifty, or even sixty. But a SPF greater than thirty offers no advantage. Here's why: An SPF of fifteen blocks out 93 percent of the ultraviolet B (UVB) rays, while an SPF of thirty blocks out more than 96 percent. But higher value SPF products provide only a minimal benefit. For example, increasing the SPF from thirty to forty increases UVB protection less than 1 percent but may require 25 percent more active ingredients.

These products usually cost more and may increase the risk for adverse effects. That's why I recommend at least an SPF fifteen sunscreen for most guys. But for those who are more sensitive to the sun, an SPF of thirty should be plenty.

Also, don't forget that the SPF ratings only apply to UVB protection. UVA rays are less likely to burn, but they penetrate deeper into the skin and lead to wrinkles, sagging, discoloration, and photosensitivity reactions over time, and UVA also contributes to skin cancer. So I tell my patients to buy a "full" or "broad-spectrum" sunscreen that protects against UVA and UVB rays.

But the Lord said to Samuel, "Do not consider his appearance or his height, for I have rejected him. The Lord does not look at the things man looks at. Man looks at the outward appearance, but the Lord looks at the heart." *1 Samuel 16:7*

My son, pay attention to what I say; turn your ear to my words. Do not let them out of your sight, keep them within your heart; for they are life to those who find them and health to one's whole body. *Proverbs 4:20–22*

Bloody Zit

Late last decade, the largest convenience store in Canada came out with a brilliant new frozen drink. Okay, brilliant is the wrong word (except the color was a brilliant red). I think *gross* is the word I'm looking for. It was called "Bloody Zit."

While adults were grossed out by the concoction, teens flooded the stores and sales skyrocketed. Kids couldn't wait to get a taste of Bloody Zit. Marketing experts called it genius. Here's why.

Teens have been making jokes about zits for years. Everybody has to deal with acne in one way or another. So kids could drink a gross-looking drink and laugh about a problem that everybody goes through.

Just one thing: Bloody Zit had a lot of sugar. And as you just read in Question 9, too much sugar in your diet is a bad thing. Sadly (or fortunately, depending on how you look at it), the Bloody Zit phenomena lasted only a short time and the drink went away — too bad our zits can't do the same thing.

QUESTION 12

Will I ever get facial hair?

I remember asking this question when I was a young man. I was worried that I would *never* have *any* facial hair or chest hair. I was jealous of my friends who did. I wondered, *Am I abnormal?*

At my school, some of my friends started shaving when they were twelve or thirteen years old—I didn't start shaving until I was almost seventeen! Because of this, I can still remember an event that happened more than forty years ago.

When I was fifteen, I walked into the school cafeteria. My friend James sat at a table with some of the jocks, talking to one of the football coaches. I sat at the next table and listened in on their conversation.

Coach Ruiz and James were talking about growing sideburns.

I couldn't believe it. I had no facial hair at all. James was not only shaving, but he could have grown a mustache! He had hair on his chest and arms and legs. I looked like a naked mole rat.

I remember how immature I felt that day—and how badly I wanted to have hair where there was none! So here is a chart on when to expect the development of hair on places besides your head:

	Early Developer	Average Boy	Late Bloomer
First fine pubic hair	Age 9	Age 12.5	Age 14
Beginning underarm and facial hair	Age 11	Age 14-15	Age 17
Coarser, longer pubic hair	Age 12	Age 14	Age 17-18
Adult-type pubic hair	Age 14	Age 16	Age 18
Facial hair thick enough to shave	Age 14	Age 16	Age 19

Remember these are just average ages. Development between young men is highly variable. Just to give you an idea:

- Some young men begin growing pubic hair at age nine; others don't see pubic hair until thirteen or fourteen.
- The development and amount of facial hair is partly determined by genetics, hormones, and race. Some young men have heavy beards; others have sparse facial hair.
- Some guys start shaving in middle school; others are razor-free into their twenties.

Also, there's almost nothing you can do to look more manly. So don't fall for any of those Internet-based treatments that claim to help you grow more facial hair at a younger age. If you buy that junk, the only thing that will grow is that company's bank account.

If you develop early, you should know that shaving does not cause your facial hair to grow more. The increase in hair growth is caused by the change and increase in hormones. The part of the hair that you see and shave is dead.

If you want a gauge of when and how much hair you'll grow, ask your father or other older males in your family at what age they started growing their beards. Do the men in your family have full beards, and when did they develop them? This may give you a good clue to the traits you may have inherited.

As I've said before, God has designed a great deal of variation in perfectly normal young men. Nevertheless, if you are concerned about whether your growth and development is normal, be sure to see your doctor.

Now let me finish the story about James and Coach Ruiz. What I didn't know until James and I talked at a high school reunion many years later was that James was embarrassed that he had too much hair. So both he and I thought we were abnormal! I felt weird for having too little hair. James felt weird for having too much. Yet the fact is that every boy develops differently.

> As for those who were held in high esteem — whatever they were makes no difference to me; God does not show favoritism.   *Galatians 2:6*

> Dear friend, I pray that you may enjoy good health and that all may go well with you, even as your soul is getting along well.
>
> *3 John 12*

Hairy Competition

You've probably heard of the Super Bowl, World Series, or Stanley Cup playoffs. But there's a competition that's hairier and even more manly than all of those put together. It's the World Beard and Moustache Championships (WBMC).

Since 1995, the WBMC have been held every two years to recognize the best facial hair on the planet. The competition is divided into seventeen categories: eight for moustaches, four for partial beards or goatees, and five for full beards.

At the 2009 championships in Anchorage, Alaska, the United States neatly shaved the other challengers by winning twelve of the eighteen categories. Many of the men dressed in costumes that complemented their facial hair and added a laugh or two.

Jack Passion defended his title in the largest category — Natural Full Beard. More than 140 other competitors were hoping to knock Jack from the top. They couldn't do it. And the amazing thing is that Jack's just twenty-five years old. (He first won the title at age twenty-three.) Some of the other competitors joked that they'd been growing their beards longer than Jack had been alive.

The overall champion was Alaska's David Traver, who shaped his twenty-inch beard into the shape of a snowshoe. He earned first place in the Full Beard Freestyle competition. Then he was awarded the competition's top prize.

Who knows, once you start getting some peach fuzz on your chin, you could join one of the fifty beard and moustache clubs in the United States. Thirty other countries boast facial hair clubs too!

QUESTION 13

Diamonds vs. sterling, are body piercings bad?

As you grow into a man, you may want to exhibit your own individual style. Some boys choose body piercing. First, you should know that body piercing is illegal for minors in most states. Furthermore, body-piercing practices are virtually unregulated in America. Since body piercing has become popular, shops have sprung up everywhere—with little or no regulation. There is very little incentive for most of these shop owners to take precautions against infections or other health hazards.

Because of these facts, experts, such as the American Academy of Dermatology, have taken a position against all forms of body piercing with one exception: the ear lobe. The American

Dental Association (ADA) opposes oral (tongue, lip, or cheek) piercing. The ADA even calls it a public health hazard!

Why? Piercing parts of your body other than your ear lobe is risky for a number of reasons.

The U.S. and Canadian Red Cross will not accept blood donations from anyone who has had a body piercing within a year. Why? Because these procedures can pass along diseases that are spread via blood—such as Hepatitis B and Hepatitis C. There are no cures for these viral illnesses that can harm your liver and even be fatal.

Other risks of having a body part pierced are:

- Infection
- Scarring (especially facial tissues like around the lips or eyes)
- Skin allergies to the jewelry that's used
- Boils (infections under the skin)
- Permanent holes or deforming scars in your nose or eyebrow
- Chipped or broken teeth (in the case of tongue piercing)
- A speech impediment (while the tongue jewelry is in place)
- And, rarely, tetanus or AIDS

If all this is true, then why is it okay to get the ear lobe pierced? Well, unlike the other areas that kids get pierced, the ear lobe is made of fatty tissue and has a great blood supply. These factors are known to protect you in the event of an infection. In addition, most shops that pierce ears use sterile piercing guns and use needles once and then dispose of them in a special container.

So think long and hard before you get anything other than

your ears pierced. You'll need a parent's permission and signature, so talk it over. If your parents say to wait until you're older, trust that they have good reasons. There are not only the physical risks of having a body piercing, but social and emotional ones too. For example, many adults make negative value judgments about people with piercings. These judgments may not be correct, but they could prevent you from getting a job down the road.

Do you not know that your bodies are temples of the Holy Spirit, who is in you, whom you have received from God? You are not your own; you were bought at a price. Therefore honor God with your bodies. *1 Corinthians 6:19-20*

I eagerly expect and hope that I will in no way be ashamed, but will have sufficient courage so that now as always Christ will be exalted in my body, whether by life or by death.

Philippians 1:20

Piercing Truth

As a little kid, you may have played "Ring Around the Rosy." Well, on March 4, 2006, Kam Ma played ring all over his upper body. For nearly eight hours, Kam allowed Charlie Wilson to put more than 1,000 skin rings in his arms to set a body-piercing record. Needless to say, Kam wasn't planning on flying anywhere, because he would've driven the metal-detecting machines crazy.

Speaking of crazy, there's a man who lives in Havana, Cuba, that has more than 300 holes in his face, and he fills them all with metal — mainly hoops. He may have more permanent piercings than any other man on the planet.

Thomas Blackthorne of the United Kingdom doesn't have many piercings, but he has one famous one — right through the middle of his tongue! Thomas puts a hook through it and lifts heavy objects. On August 1, 2008, Thomas set a world record for most weight lifted by the human tongue at 27 pounds and 8.96 ounces. To be fair, his tongue really didn't "lift" the weight. After attaching his tongue to the massive weight, Thomas carefully used his legs to get the weight off the ground. His tongue just held the weight without being torn in two or ripped out of his mouth. *Gross!*

Kids ... don't try any of these things at home.

QUESTION 14

Under my skin, how about tattoos?

With so many professional athletes and movie stars sporting tattoos, you may think it's a cool idea to get one someday. But if you're thinking about getting a tattoo, think very carefully. First of all, it's illegal for minors to be tattooed in most states, which have laws prohibiting tattooing on minors without written parental consent.

Tattooing is a very painful process. Once done, if you change your mind, tattoos are even more painful to remove (and very expensive). And removing tattoos often leaves ugly scars.

Worse yet, tattooing involves health risks. In most states, tattoo parlors are not regulated. Unclean equipment, ink, or technique can infect you with a lifelong, incurable infection—such as HIV, the virus that causes AIDS, or Hepatitis B or C, which causes liver failure, liver cancer, or even premature death. Because of the risk of these infections, the American Association of Blood Banks won't accept blood donations until one year after a person has received a tattoo to see if an infection will show up. And it is now recommended that physicians screen all of their patients with a tattoo for Hepatitis C, because everyone who has a tattoo is at risk for being infected with this virus.

Skin infection is another possible side effect of tattoos — especially local bacterial infections. Normally skin infections are characterized by redness, swelling, pain, and a pus-like drainage, but one of the worst skin infections doctors see with tattooing is called *community-associated methicillin-resistant Staphylococcus aureus*, or CA-MRSA infection. MRSA is dangerous because these bacteria are resistant to most antibiotics.

These infections are contracted because of unsanitary tattoo equipment and unsafe practices used by unlicensed tattoo artists, some of whom use guitar strings in lieu of needles and ink from printer cartridges rather than tattoo ink.

Tattooing can also lead to other skin problems. Sometimes bumps, called *granulomas,* form around tattoo ink — especially red ink. Tattooing can also lead to raised areas caused by an overgrowth of scar tissue (keloids).

Other risks from tattoos include chronic skin irritation that can occur for years. Some of the dyes used in tattooing are not even approved for use in humans!

According to the Mayo Clinic, in some rare cases, tattoos or permanent makeup may cause swelling or burning in the affected areas during magnetic resonance imaging (MRI) exams. Plus, the tattoo pigments may interfere with the quality of the image.

Although it's rare, some people have allergic reactions to the tattoo pigments. These reactions can be severe and cause terrible ulcers or scarring.

Last, but not least, I've seen patients with severe scarring from both tattooing and tattoo removal.

The saddest side effect of a tattoo is regret. I can't count the number of people I've taken care of who wish they had thought twice. Never get a tattoo without giving yourself time (weeks, months, or even years) to think and pray about it. Talk to your parents and friends. Double-check your motives with someone you admire and trust.

As a follower of Jesus, there are a number of commands in the Scripture about obeying your parents. Since you are under their roof, their care, and their authority, if they oppose you having a tattoo or a body piercing, then going ahead and doing it is a sin.

> Children, obey your parents in the Lord, for this is right. "Honor your father and mother"—which is the first commandment with a promise—"so that it may go well with you and that you may enjoy long life on the earth." *Ephesians 6:1-3*

> Honor your father and your mother, so that you may live long in the land the Lord your God is giving you. *Exodus 20:12*

So seriously and prayerfully consider the physical, relational, social, and emotional risks of having a body piercing or a tattoo. Ask yourself these questions:

- Why is it that I am considering this?
- How does my motive and desire line up with what the Bible teaches?
- What is my heart and conscience saying to me?
- Is the Holy Spirit telling me to do this or convicting me not to?
- Do I have freedom in Christ and a clear conscience before the Lord regarding this decision?

- Am I a hundred percent sure I'll still want this tattoo or piercing years from now?
- Will my future wife approve?
- Will I cause a weaker brother to stumble if I get a piercing or tattoo?

One of my teen reviewers wrote, "I think it would be helpful to remind young men that if they plan to marry in the future, it is important to remember that their body actually will belong to their spouse, and many young ladies do not like tattoos."

Perhaps the most important question of all is the one that a teen reviewer for this book asks himself, "Am I considering doing this for God's glory, or my glory?" Great question!

> Do not cut your bodies for the dead or put tattoo marks on yourselves. I am the Lord. *Leviticus 19:28*

I know there are those who say that since this is Levitical Law it doesn't apply to Christians. However, in this same section of the law are admonitions to "not practice divination or sorcery," to "not turn to mediums or seek out spiritualists, for you will be defiled by them," to "not degrade your daughter by making her a prostitute," and to "observe my Sabbaths and have reverence for my sanctuary. I am the Lord."

> Children, obey your parents in everything, for this pleases the Lord. *Colossians 3:20*

> … Everything that does not come from faith is sin. *Romans 14:23*

Stinkin' Inkin'

TV shows about tattoo parlors can make tattooing look like a cool, fresh way to express your individualism. But the truth is tattooing has been around for thousands of years. Some scientists say they've found tattoos on ice men who lived 3,000 years before Jesus walked the earth. Others say tattoos have been discovered on Egyptian mummies that date back to 2000 BC.

Today, a lot of people have gotten carried away with tattoos. One guy tattooed himself to look like a leopard. Another inked up to look like a zebra. Then there's a lizard man, and a man who got tattoos that look like a skeleton.

But nobody can say they've had as many tattoos as Australia's Lucky Diamond Rich. In 2006 he earned the title of world's most tattooed person when he had his entire body tattooed with black ink — even between his toes, on his eyelids, and inside his ears! Now he's having white tattoo designs put over the black ones and colored tattoos put over the white.

In all, he's spent more than one thousand hours having his appearance modified.

QUESTION 15

Temporary vs. permanent, are tattoos safe?

When I say "temporary tattoo" I'm not talking about the kind you put on with a wet wash cloth, I'm referring to the so-called temporary tattoos that are usually made with black henna and are meant to fade over several days or weeks. Black henna tattoos are especially popular with teens and can often be found at coastal beach shops and in tourist areas.

Since henna application does not puncture the skin, it is not technically defined as a tattoo, and so it's not regulated. (Tattooing is defined as placing a permanent mark on the skin through the insertion of pigment or dye into the skin.) Compared to tattoos, henna marking on the skin poses almost no risk of hepatitis, AIDS, and many of the other more serious health risks associated with traditional tattoos. But every year the Department of Health in Florida receives dozens of reports from children and adults with severe allergic reactions from temporary black henna tattoos they got while vacationing. In fact, the U.S. Food and Drug Administration (FDA) does not approve henna for direct application to the skin. Henna, a coloring made from a plant, is approved only for use as a hair dye.

Henna alone typically produces a brown or orange-brown tint, so other ingredients must be added to make different colors, such as those marketed as black henna — which can contain a chemical called *coal tar color para-phenylenediamine*, also known as PPD.

The PPD pigment is known to cause mild to serious allergic reactions when it is applied directly to the skin. The problem is that most people don't know if they are allergic to it until they have already received lasting damage from a reaction.

Just like other chemicals that cause allergies, such as bee stings or nuts, PPD causes different people to react in different ways. Some have a strong or even dangerous reaction the very first time they are exposed. Others may have a mild reaction or none at all, but become sensitized after several exposures.

Once you become sensitized to PPD, the allergy is permanent — it is life long — and can lead to reactions to other common items such as black clothing, sunscreens, hair dye, and even the numbing medicine benzocaine.

And on rare occasions, the skin reaction to PPD can be so severe that it burns and blisters the skin, leaving permanent scarring. A number of people have filed lawsuits against distributors of black henna after their children were scarred from receiving black henna tattoos.

Although most boys won't experience a problem, some could be permanently scarred with a permanent reminder of a "temporary" poor decision. At the very least, if you want a temporary henna tattoo, make sure you avoid "black henna."

May God himself, the God of peace, sanctify you through and through. May your whole spirit, soul and body be kept blameless at the coming of our Lord Jesus Christ.

1 Thessalonians 5:23

So whether you eat or drink or whatever you do, do it all for the glory of God.   *1 Corinthians 10:31*

Henna Horror Stories

Seven-year-old Joseph just wanted to get a fun seahorse temporary tattoo to remember his family's trip to the beach during the summer of 2010. Now he has a permanent raised, reddish, seahorse-shaped scar on his right arm.

Sixteen-year-old Christopher paid forty dollars to get three temporary star tattoos on his back. Hours later, the stars caused shooting pains, blistered, and began weeping pus. The wounds were so bad that Christopher had to change his T-shirt five times a day. When he returned home from vacation, his doctor recommended plastic surgery to help with the permanent scars. Friends thought Christopher had been branded. Not only did the temporary tattoo ruin Christopher's vacation, it also cost his family a lot of time and money.

QUESTION 16

What if my friends try alcohol?

A lot of boys I talk to don't know that alcohol in any form (wine, beer, or liquor) is a drug—an *illegal* drug if you're under twenty-one years of age. So, for those of us professing to be Christians, this means underage drinking is a sin because it breaks the law. For a lot of young men, this is enough to help them decide alcohol isn't worth the trouble.

Another lesser-known fact to consider, did you know it's easier to become addicted to alcohol when you're younger? A Substance Abuse and Mental Health Services Administration survey found that youth who start drinking before age fifteen are five times more likely to have problems with alcohol later in life than those who began drinking at twenty-one or older.

Addiction to alcohol is known as *alcoholism*, and people with this addiction are called *alcoholics*. Alcoholism is a terrible enslavement in every way—physically, emotionally, relationally, and spiritually—and it is totally preventable.

The Bible teaches that as Christians we are to be wise and cautious in how we live. We are *not* to be foolish, and we are *not* to get drunk:

> Follow God's example....
>
> Be very careful, then, how you live—not as unwise but as wise....
>
> Therefore do not be foolish, but understand what the Lord's will is.
>
> Do not get drunk on wine, which leads to debauchery. Instead, be filled with the Spirit. *Ephesians 5:1, 15, 17-18*

To be "filled with the Spirit" means to be controlled by, to be directed by, and to be empowered by the Spirit of God himself. As such, we are to be self-controlled, not out of control.

> You are all children of the light and children of the day. We do not belong to the night or to the darkness. So then, let us not be like others, who are asleep, but let us be awake and sober. For those who sleep, sleep at night, and those who get drunk, get drunk at night. But since we belong to the day, let us be sober, putting on faith and love as a breastplate, and the hope of salvation as a helmet.
>
> *1 Thessalonians 5:5-8*

I find in my medical practice that people who drink alcohol, whether young or old, seem to have the same lame excuses for excessive drinking. As you get older, you'll probably notice that when it comes to drug use—including alcohol, marijuana, prescription drugs, or huffing (sniffing various chemicals or glue)—

you'll hear a lot of the same things from people who want to get you to try them. Here are just a few of the lies about drugs that you may hear from your friends:

Lie No. 1: "Alcohol will help you deal with your problems."

The truth is many people use alcohol as a drug to numb their pain. They use it to escape from problems or to forget their troubles. But guess what? When the effect of the drug wears off, all of their problems are still there. And many times there are even more problems caused by the drinking. Alcohol never, ever, ever helps solve what is wrong with your life. In fact, it almost always makes things worse.

Lie No. 2: "Drinking will make you look cool."

This may be one of the biggest lies of all about alcohol. The truth is people who drink do incredibly uncool things — like stumbling or falling, slurring their speech, having accidents, saying things that hurt others, vomiting their guts out, losing control of their behavior, and many other stupid things.

Worse yet, teens who drink and drive end up killing or injuring themselves or others almost every day of the year. Each year, thousands of fifteen- to twenty-year-old drivers are killed in alcohol-related motor vehicle accidents, while nearly 300,000 are injured.

Lie No. 3: "Drinking alcohol will make you happy and help you have a good time."

No doubt about it, drinking alcohol will give you a "buzz" — especially when the alcohol first begins to affect your brain. It's a form of intoxication not only of the brain, but of your entire nervous system. However, alcohol never makes a person happy. Alcohol as a drug is a depressant. Therefore, it tends to make most people feel down and drowsy — to move and react much more slowly than usual and to be depressed after it wears off.

At first, someone who's drinking alcohol might seem to lose their inhibitions — in other words, they "loosen up" and do or say things they normally wouldn't. This is why some people seem "wild" or "out of control" when they drink. But the truth is even if someone seems "pumped up" when they drink, the alcohol always ends up making them sluggish, slow, and unable to make wise decisions.

Experts who work with adolescent sex offenders who were drinking or on drugs when they committed the offense often hear the perpetrator say, "It was the alcohol," or "It was the drugs." But these experts say the alcohol does not make a person do anything they don't want to do, but does make it easier for a person to cross the boundaries on what they know is right and wrong. You are more likely not to think of the consequences for doing something when you are drinking or high on other illegal drugs.

Lie No. 4: "If you just drink beer or wine and avoid hard liquor, you won't get drunk or become an alcoholic."

Totally false. The fact is beer, wine, and hard liquor all contain the exact same drug: alcohol!

A lot of boys I've worked with have told me that they tried alcohol or drugs because their friends were doing it. The pressure of your friends can be overwhelming—and not just to drink alcohol, but to use or take any drug that is not prescribed for you by your doctor, whether legal or illegal.

In school and in the neighborhood, in clubs and on teams—even in church youth group—you will feel peer pressure to do wrong things. But it's never right to do what's wrong, is it? There are *always* consequences for doing wrong things—there's always a price to pay. Sometimes that price can be very, very high.

Think about it for a moment. If you are tempted to drink because your friends want you to or are pushing you to, then it's time to ask a very important question: What would happen if you told them you weren't interested in drinking alcohol?

Would your friends not want to hang out with you anymore because of your decision? And if they did, were they really true friends in the first place?

Of course not. A real friend, a true friend, will respect your decisions—always.

Here are some great tips about handling the pressure to try alcohol or other drugs:

- You don't have to do anything that you don't want to do.
- You should not do anything that is not right to do.
- Giving in to peer pressure never solves problems or makes people like and respect you more.

The Bible teaches that with each temptation that comes our way, God provides a *way of escape*:

> No temptation has overtaken you except what is common to mankind. And God is faithful; he will not let you be tempted beyond what you can bear. But when you are tempted, he will also provide a way out so that you can endure it. *1 Corinthians 10:13*

"But," you may ask, "how can I escape the temptation—the pressure?" Remember, it's always okay to just say "no." You don't have to give a reason. You don't have to explain yourself. You don't have to use your faith as an excuse.

If you're offered alcohol, you can suggest an alternative: "I think I'd rather have a soda" or something like that.

Of course, choosing to do something that is wrong may be pleasurable for a brief period of time ... but it will always catch up with you. There's always a price to pay.

If you've already fallen to temptation with alcohol or other drugs, know that your Savior, Jesus (who faced many temptations), understands completely and wants you to talk to him and tap into his power.

> For we do not have a high priest who is unable to empathize with our weaknesses, but we have one who has been tempted in every way, just as we are—yet he did not sin. Let us then approach God's throne of grace with confidence, so that we may receive mercy and find grace to help us in our time of need. *Hebrews 4:15-16*

As an example of the power of faith in helping to make the right choice, think about the life of Moses. When he was a young man, Moses was tempted to do a number of things that were wrong. But he chose not to. The Bible tells us about his example:

> By faith Moses, when he had grown up, refused to be known as the son of Pharaoh's daughter. He chose to be mistreated along with the people of God rather than to enjoy the fleeting pleasures of sin. He regarded disgrace for the sake of Christ as of greater value than the treasures of Egypt, because he was looking ahead to his reward. By faith he left Egypt, not fearing the king's anger; he persevered because he saw him who is invisible.
>
> *Hebrews 11:24-25*

Notice, Moses was able to make the right decision "by faith." His faith became a resource — a strength for him in choosing right over wrong.

Today, God gives his children the gift of the Holy Spirit to guide us in making the right decisions.

I know saying "no" isn't always easy. But by standing strong, you may find that many of your friends secretly feel the same way you do! They'll likely respect you even more because they know deep down that you are doing the right thing. It may even give them the courage to also say "no." You can be an important positive influence in your friends' lives! It takes courage to do what is right, even if it is "uncool."

But if you continue to get pressured, talk about it with your dad or another trusted adult.

> Wine is a mocker and beer a brawler; whoever is led astray by them is not wise. *Proverbs 20:1*

> Don't drink too much wine. That cheapens your life. Drink the Spirit of God, huge draughts of him. Sing hymns instead of drinking songs! Sing songs from your heart to

Christ. Sing praises over everything, any excuse for a song
to God the Father in the name of our Master, Jesus Christ.

Ephesians 5:18-20 MSG

"Everybody's Doing It"

At a point in your life (maybe it's already
happened to you), someone will challenge you to
do something with the words "Everybody's doing it." The
temptation might come in the form of shoplifting, going
too far sexually, or trying drugs or alcohol. But no matter
what the temptation is, know this fact: everybody is *not*
doing it.

When it comes to alcohol, studies show that nearly 60
percent of twelve- to seventeen-year-olds have never had
a drink. That proves a lot of youth are saying no. Because
the same study found that more than 60 percent of eighth
graders said alcohol was "fairly easy" or "very easy" to get.

Experimenting with alcohol can be dangerous, but trying other illegal drugs can be even more dangerous or
even fatal. Taking somebody else's prescription pills, huffing, or trying harder drugs, such as cocaine, can kill a
person the first time they try them. If you're ever tempted
to take drugs, remember the story of Len Bias.

"Who?" you may ask. Have you ever heard of Michael
Jordan or Dwayne Wade? Well, Len was believed by basketball experts to have the skill and talent of those two NBA
greats. But shortly after being drafted with the number two
overall pick in the 1986 NBA draft, Len died of a cocaine
overdose. Many people believe, including his mother, that
this was the first time Len experimented with drugs. The
six-feet-seven-inch, 221-pound forward had all the talent

in the world. He could soar to the basket and throw down thunderous dunks, or step back and nail long jump shots. His future seemed limitless. Yet at age twenty-two, he lay dead in a casket after the cocaine in his body caused his heart to stop. Len had never failed a drug test. Yet one night of partying and a bad decision cost him his life.

So even if "everybody's doing it" when it comes to alcohol and drugs, weigh the consequences, turn to Jesus to make the right decision, and walk away from the crowd.

QUESTION 17

My breasts are growing! What's wrong with me?

Nothing! This is not some malformity. It's just God's design at work in you.

Everyone knows that enlarged breasts are supposed to grow on girls, right? Right. But what most people don't know is that during puberty up to 60 percent of all boys will temporarily have a bit of breast growth and tenderness. Just know you are not turning into a girl, and you will not need to wear a bra.

We doctors call this normal phase of breast growth *gynecomastia* (pronounced guy-neh-coh-mass-tee-uh).

In the beginning stages of puberty, there are all kinds of hormonal changes that occur in your body. This flood of hormones is believed to cause the breast tissue to develop. For most of the guys with breast growth, there will also be some tenderness. Sometimes both breasts will develop small growths under the nipple, but for most young men, it will occur on only one breast.

If this happens to you, don't worry. Your breasts will not continue to grow like a girl's breasts will. A young man's breast growth, which usually starts before fourteen years of age, is almost always temporary. The growth will usually disappear — although it can take up to three years to resolve (most of the time it's less than two years).

Nevertheless, if either you or your parents are concerned about gynecomastia, be sure to have your doctor take a look. He or she can do a very brief exam and usually put your mind at ease. Remember, although this may be embarrassing for you, this is everyday stuff for your doctor.

Also, keep in mind that although you are feeling *very* self-conscious and weird about this, most of your male friends are probably going through exactly the same thing!

Your breast growth or tenderness can become another way for you to thank God that he's begun to take you through puberty. This process is necessary for him to grow you into the powerful man of God that he wants you to become.

> Whatever you do, work at it with all your heart, as working for the Lord, not for human masters, since you know that you will receive an inheritance from the Lord as a reward. It is the Lord Christ you are serving. *Colossians 3:23-24*

Breast Reduction

A recent study of nearly 1,700 fourteen- and fifteen-year-olds found that young men with high levels of lead in their blood had a greater chance of experiencing increased breast growth, known as gynecomastia. While this condition normally goes away on its own after a couple of years, some extreme cases have required surgery.

If you're experiencing this, here are a few ideas to help you through:

- Wear loose-fitting shirts to help make gynecomastia less noticeable and decrease the tenderness.
- Avoid rubbing your breasts — as it can increase the growth and the time it takes your breasts to shrink to normal size.
- Avoid using a heating pad or taking long soaks in a hot tub as this can also make the problem worse.

QUESTION 18

Is having only one testicle okay?

Well, it's not normal, but it's also not rare. In fact, a number of well-known men have been reported to have only one testicle, including Spanish dictator General Francisco Franco, French emperor Napoleon Bonaparte, former California governor Arnold Schwarzenegger, seven-time Tour de France winner Lance Armstrong, Red Sox third baseman Mike Lowell, Idaho senator Frank Church, and Olympic Gold Medalist and World Champion ice skater Scott Hamilton.

I have no idea if the reports about these men's *monorchism* (the medical term for having only one testicle) are accurate or not, but I do know that for a young man, having a single testicle can be a source of great embarrassment.

Let me pass along some facts to you about his situation. There are a number of reasons a male may have one testicle:

- For some boys, one of the testicles may disappear during development in his mother's womb. This is called a *vanishing testicle*.
- One testicle may have been surgically removed through a procedure called *orchiectomy*. This may be required because of an injury, or an infection, or because one of the testes had cancer.
- In other cases, one of the testicles may not have descended from the abdomen into the scrotum during normal development before birth. This can be seen in 3 to 4 percent of normal live births. This is called *undescended testis* or *cryptorchidism*.

When your Creator was forming you in your mother's womb, the testicles start their formation within the abdominal cavity. Over time, they descend through the inguinal canal and into the scrotum. If that descent fails, the testicle will remain in the abdomen or the inguinal canal and is at increased risk for cancer — thus requiring surgery.

Nevertheless, God has wonderfully made us. When a boy loses one testicle, the remaining testicle will produce extra male hormone (testosterone) and more than enough sperm. The extra testicle will even grow a bit larger to support this extra production.

For cosmetic reasons, and to keep other boys from kidding or making fun of him, doctors can place an artificial testicle in the scrotum so that its appearance looks normal.

A guy with one testicle is just as much a man as a guy with two testicles. However, in most states, a boy with one testicle (or one eye or one kidney) cannot participate in contact sports without special permission from his parents and his doctor. This is in order to protect the remaining testicle for the future and avoid an injury that would cause permanent damage to the only testicle.

> How precious to me are your thoughts, God! How vast is the sum of them! Were I to count them, they would outnumber the grains of sand. When I awake, I am still with you.
>
> *Psalm 139:17-18*

Rocky Mountain Oysters

Having one testicle is normal, but rare. Eating the testicles of a male cow is also normal, but rare. It's true.

Known as Rocky Mountain oysters, prairie oysters, or calf fries, bull testicles are considered a delicacy in ranching communities in the United States, Canada, Mexico, and Spain. In fact, since May 1993, the small town of Throckmorton, Texas, has held the World Championship Rocky Mountain Oyster Festival. In the first year of the festival, fifteen teams participated in a cook-off with nearly 1,500 attending the event.

Rocky Mountain oysters are often deep fried, but can be served a variety of ways. In addition to festivals and some specialty restaurants, Rocky Mountain oysters can often be found at Coors Field during Colorado Rockies baseball games.

Wonder what they taste like? Chicken, of course!

My testicles itch and look strange, is that normal?

It is completely normal for testicles to be different sizes. This is just part of your normal development as a young man. Also, the testicles lie at different heights in the scrotum, which sometimes accentuates the size difference.

However, if your scrotum itches a lot every day, especially if there's a reddish rash, it can indicate a problem called *jock itch*. This problem occurs when a fungal infection grows on the skin of the scrotum.

The symptoms of jock itch include:

- Itching (thus the name) and sometimes burning or pain on the skin around the scrotum.
- Rash on the scrotum, inner thighs, or buttocks. The rash usually does not occur on the penis.

- The edge of the rash is very distinct and may be scaly or have bumps that look like blisters.
- The center of the rash may either have a red-brown color or even appear normal.

Jock itch (also called *tinea cruris*) is a form of ringworm, which is *not* caused by an actual worm. Rather, it is an infection of the outer layers of skin by fungi, which are microscopic organisms. It's called *ringworm* because as the infection moves outward it appears to form a ring.

Fungi are normally present on the surface and top layer of our skin. But when conditions are just right, fungus can grow beyond a normal amount and cause infection. The same fungi causes both jock itch and athlete's foot (also called *tinea pedis*).

Fungi tend to grow best in warm, moist areas of the body such as the groin, inner thighs, buttocks, and feet. Since fungi are commonly found in warm, humid rooms as well as on damp towels, sweaty workout clothes, and wet floors, it's not surprising that jock itch and athlete's foot often occur at the same time.

Although jock itch is bothersome and annoying, it is not a serious problem. It can, however, recur. But once you've had jock itch in the past, you'll almost always recognize it when it returns.

Here's one quick etiquette reminder for you: try to be careful not to scratch this area when you are around other people — especially young women. This can be very embarrassing to them.

Your doctor can tell if you have jock itch by asking you a few questions about your symptoms, examining your rash, and possibly scraping it so that he or she can look at it under a microscope. Other times the doctor may rub the rash with a small brush in order to do a culture test to see if fungi are present. Both procedures are completely painless.

Ringworm infections of the skin, including jock itch and athlete's foot, can be treated at home with inexpensive, over-the-counter antifungal creams.

To treat jock itch, follow these steps:

- Wash the rash with soap and water and dry well. Spread an antifungal cream over the rash. Apply the cream beyond the edge of the rash.
- Use an antifungal cream that contains terbinafine, miconazole, or clotrimazole. You can buy these products without a prescription. Brand names include Lamisil AT, Lotrimin, Micatin, and Monistat.
- Follow the directions on the package, and don't stop using the medicine just because your symptoms go away. In other words, use the medication for the full time indicated on the product label. The itching and rash will likely improve before the infection under the skin is completely cured.
- If the symptoms do not improve after two weeks, call your doctor to set up an appointment.

If you have jock itch *and* athlete's foot, you should *treat both* at the same time to prevent reinfecting your groin when you put on your underwear.

Preventing jock itch and athlete's foot is fairly easy. It starts by keeping your groin, inner thighs, buttocks, and feet clean and dry. Be sure to dry off well after you workout, exercise, or shower. Wash your workout clothes and towels frequently — and wash your underwear, jock straps or athletic cups and socks after each use. Wearing shower shoes when you use public showers and locker rooms is also a good idea.

In addition, always dry your feet last when you towel off after a shower or bath. This helps prevent spreading an infection from your feet to your groin.

> For my loins are full of inflammation...
>
> *Psalm 38:7 NKJV*

Okay, just kidding … this verse is not about jock itch, but I thought you'd find it funny.

> I'm an open book to you; even from a distance, you know what I'm thinking.
> You know when I leave and when I get back; I'm never out of your sight.
> You know everything I'm going to say before I start the first sentence.
> I look behind me and you're there, then up ahead and you're there, too — your reassuring presence, coming and going.
> This is too much, too wonderful — I can't take it all in!
>
> *Psalm 139:2 – 6 MSG*

Itchy and Scratchy

While it can feel embarrassing to have jock itch or athlete's foot, both conditions are very normal … and treatable. Which do you think is more common, jock itch or athlete's foot? The answer is jock itch.

Seventy-five percent of men will experience jock itch at some point in their lives. Athlete's foot affects 15 percent of the general population, while 20 percent of men sixteen years or older contract the fungi.

Why do doctors
check my testicles?

Physical exams,
whether they are
for a pre-school exam, a
sports exam, or a camp
exam, are usually pretty
straightforward. Doctors
do them every day.

But you may wonder,
"Why does the doctor need
to feel my testicles and make me
cough?" It can seem pretty embarrassing, and you may say, "Isn't there
a less-awkward way for the doctor to check
things out?"

When you have a physical exam, the doctor is interested in
finding out about your overall health. This requires that the doctor check your height and weight and take your blood pressure.
The doctor will listen to your heart, lungs, and abdomen. The
doctor will look at your eyes, ears, nose, and throat. The doctor

should test your back and joints to be sure they are healthy and test your reflexes by tapping your knees and ankles.

However, for some parts of your body, the doctor must rely on his or her sense of touch and training in knowing how things should feel. We call this *palpation*. During the exam, he or she will touch or palpate your abdomen and move and stretch your joints.

Your doctor may also feel your neck, armpits, and groin to detect if there is any abnormal swelling. He or she should also examine your testicles and the area around them to detect any abnormalities such as a missing testicle, a hernia, or a tumor.

An inguinal hernia is a bulge in the groin area or a mass in the scrotum caused by the contents of your abdomen (for example, the intestine) pushing through a weak spot in the abdominal wall. It is important to check for a hernia so it can be treated early before it becomes a major problem. A hernia can sometimes lead to damage to your intestines, so finding it and fixing the weak spot through surgery is sometimes necessary.

It's also vital that the doctor gently check your testicles to be sure there are no abnormalities—especially cancer. Although testicular cancer is very unusual in young men (it occurs in three out of 100,000 guys between the ages of fifteen and nineteen), it is the second most common cancer seen during the teen years. For young men between twenty to thirty-four years of age, it is the most common cancer—and no one really knows why it occurs in people who are so young.

Olympic ice skating champion Scott Hamilton and seven-time Tour de France champion cyclist Lance Armstrong have both successfully won battles with testicular cancer. Finding the cancer early dramatically increases your chance of beating this disease.

The doctor will gently palpate (touch) one testicle at a time, rolling it very carefully between his or her thumb and first finger. He or she will feel for lumps and also pay attention to whether the testicle is abnormal in any way.

Your doctor should also teach *you* how to do testicular self-exams. But even if he or she does not, you should still gently examine your testicles at least once a month. I always tell the young men in my practice to do this on the first day of the month—since that's an easy day to remember. I tell them to do this while showering or bathing, as a soapy lather makes examining the testicles easier. Your testicles should feel smooth like a hard-boiled egg without a shell, and there shouldn't be any lumps or bumps. If you notice any changes to your testicle, be sure to let you parents know and have a doctor's exam immediately.

> Test me, Lord, and try me, examine my heart and my mind; for I have always been mindful of your unfailing love and have lived in reliance in your faithfulness.
>
> *Psalm 26:2-3*

> You have searched me, and you know me.   *Psalm 139:1*

Let's Get Physical

Has a doctor ever drummed on your body during a physical exam? If so, that's totally normal. It's called percussion, or tapping for signs of good health. With experience and training, doctors know how a body should sound when it's tapped on in certain places. Percussion is one of the four steps in a physical exam, and one that seems kind of funny.

Many schools, sports teams, and camps require that you receive a physical exam before participating. Physical exams provide a doctor the opportunity to check your overall health.

Normally, a physical exam includes a four-part plan. In addition to percussion, doctors should go through the steps referred to as inspection, palpation, and auscultation.

During the inspection phase, the doctor looks you over for signs of health. The doctor will palpitate or feel for abnormalities. And, of course, a doctor will listen to your heart and lungs during auscultation.

During any part of a physical exam, if you feel uncomfortable or have a question, feel free to ask. Communicating with your doctor is a great way to learn more about your body and take an active role in your overall health.

QUESTION 21

How do I know if my penis is the right size?

This is one of the most asked questions by boys your age. Every young man (and many adult men) wonders the exact same thing. So here's the scoop.

First things first: there is a very wide range of normal sizes—just as there is for every part of the body. Furthermore, just like other parts of the body, how a penis appears at different stages of a guy's life varies quite a bit.

Think about it, you wouldn't expect someone who is eleven years old to look the same as someone who's sixteen, would you?

In addition, think of the differences between the boys you know. Some are taller. Others are shorter. It's all part of the way God designed each one of us.

I've done thousands of exams on young men. As a volunteer physician for the U.S. Olympic Committee, I have examined young athletes from a wide variety of sports. And I can tell you that penises come in a variety of different sizes (from smaller to larger), shapes (from round to oval), colors (lighter to darker skin), and lengths (short to long). These traits are inherited, like eye color or foot size, and there's nothing you can do to change that.

As you progress through puberty, your penis will grow and you'll notice a bunch of other changes—such as the development of pubic hair and the growth of your testicles. You'll also grow stronger and larger muscles, get taller and heavier, and have your voice change. The size of your penis is in no way related to your masculinity or ability to father a child.

Even though it has no significance, I still have young male patients ask, "Doc, what's the average penis length?" It's a fair question.

Researchers have found (yes, they do study these things) that a non-erect penis varies from 8.5 cm to 10.5 cm (3-4 inches) from tip to base. The average is about 9.5 cm (3.75 inches).

But as I explain to my patients, this kind of measurement isn't really helpful. Many factors can cause a temporary shrinkage of two inches or more—most notably exposure to cold weather or cold water.

Many boys believe the larger or taller the man, the larger the penis. However, this is not true. In one research study, the largest penis was measured on a slim man who was only five feet seven inches tall. The smallest penis in this research study belonged to a taller and much heavier man.

Also, in every study ever published, there is no correlation between penile size and race.

Later in the book (Question 22), we'll talk more about penile erections. While we're concentrating on the size of penises, many young men are curious about how long a penis is when it's erect.

Studies show that the vast majority of men have erect penises measuring between 15 cm and 18 cm (6 to 7 inches) long. And the average is about 16.5 cm (6.5 inches).

There are no special exercises, supplements, or diets that will speed up the development process. Also, don't forget that there's a natural optical illusion. When you look at your feet, they look smaller than they really are. In the same way, your penis may look smaller to you than it really is.

If you're concerned about your penis size, don't try to compare yourself to your older brother or your best friend — they are simply at a different stage of development than you. The important thing to remember is that it's okay *not* to be exactly like your friends. Why? Because God made *you* to be unique.

> You made all the delicate, inner parts of my body and knit me together in my mother's womb. Thank you for making me so wonderfully complex! Your workmanship is marvelous — how well I know it.   *Psalm 139:13-14 NLT*

Brain Boost

Even though a lot of young men ask about it, penis size doesn't really make a difference. Here's another human body fact that doesn't make much of a difference either — the male brain is actually larger than the female brain.

Now don't go running around saying boys are smarter than girls. Studies show that on average girls actually get better grades in school than boys. But when it comes to total brain size, the average man's brain weighs about 11 percent more than a woman's. Of course, it's also good to remember that God created men with bigger heads (about

2 percent bigger), larger bodies, and greater muscle mass. Men also have 4 percent more brain cells than women.

So boys, let's all act smart. You've certainly got the brain power to do it.

QUESTION 22

Why do I get an erection when I don't want to?

An *erection* occurs when your penis fills with blood and becomes rigid. Erections are a perfectly normal bodily function and are especially common in young men who are going through puberty. The increased frequency of erections in puberty is caused by the release of testosterone.

But it can be embarrassing if an erection occurs at the wrong time. They can happen while you are doing something you particularly like or something that causes a strong emotion — such as excitement or fear. It's not uncommon for a young man to experience an erection even when he definitely doesn't want one, such as while he is swimming or sitting in church. One of my young patients told me, "My penis seems to have a mind of its own!"

Although the purpose of erections is to consummate a sexual relationship, erections can happen for no apparent reason. It's normal. There's no reason to worry that something is wrong with you. It does not indicate you are gay or becoming a sex maniac. Your body is just acting naturally for a young man your age. It's how God designed you. Having an erection is not sinful—it's a gift from God!

Many young men wonder if they are getting too many erections. Well, quite frankly, it's impossible to say what's "normal." God has created each of us uniquely. Some guys experience many erections each day, while others may have them only once or twice a week.

Your sexual hormones fluctuate wildly as a young man. They will vary depending on your age, sexual maturity, and even the amount of sleep you get. So should you worry about having "too many" erections? Not unless your erections are causing you discomfort or pain, or if your penis seems to be "bent" or "angulated." In these cases, be sure to talk to your dad, another trusted male in your life, or a doctor.

As you advance through puberty, your hormones will eventually begin to even out. At that time, the frequency of unexpected erections should decrease. Although the frequency of unwanted erections decreases as you grow into adulthood, you'll never get total control through your entire adult life. In fact, most boys and men wake up in the morning with an erection more times than not.

Even though erections are normal and natural, you should not forget that as a young man you can also be aroused sexually by what you see with your eyes or with your mind's eye—your imagination. Controlling your thoughts and what you look at can go a long way toward helping decrease the frequency of unwanted erections. Even so, erections will still remain a normal part of your life—part of God's divine design of you as a young man!

Every good and perfect gift is from above, coming down from the Father of the heavenly lights, who does not change like shifting shadows.   *James 1:17*

You watched me as I was being formed in utter seclusion, as I was woven together in the dark of the womb. You saw me before I was born. Every day of my life was recorded in your book. Every moment was laid out before a single day had passed.   *Psalm 139:15-16 NLT*

A Hard Situation

So you're sitting in school, or church, or in the movies and get an erection, what do you do? Depending on what you're wearing, you may be able to somewhat hide this embarrassing situation. If your pants are loose enough, you may be able to discreetly "tuck" your penis under the waistband. If your shirt is tucked in, you can un-tuck it and use it to cover up.

But hiding an erection can be uncomfortable and awkward. You probably want to know how to make an erection go away as soon as possible. As a growing young man with hormones flying around your body, it's nearly impossible to control when you get an erection. However, you may be able to decrease the duration of an erection by using one of the most powerful parts of your body — your brain.

By thinking about disgusting or boring things, you may be able to help your penis shrink back to its normal state. Can you remember a time that you were really sick? Perfect! How about when a teammate of yours vomited on the field after running wind sprints? That could work. What's your least favorite food? Think about that. Or try picturing a rolling river cutting through a wheat field that's gently swaying in the breeze.

While your penis may have a "mind of its own," the brain between your ears can help you avoid some potentially embarrassing situations. Just think about it!

QUESTION 23

What is a wet dream?

When guys go through puberty, they will begin having what are commonly called *wet dreams*. The technical name for a wet dream is *nocturnal emission*. *Nocturnal* means *at night*, and *emission* means *discharge*.

During the part of sleep in which dreams most commonly occur, guys can have erections and then discharge a few drops of semen (the fluid containing sperm from the testicles and fluid from the reproductive glands). This forms a wet, sticky spot on your underwear or pajamas. This is not urine, but a wet dream.

This can be embarrassing and even confusing if you do not know what is happening. The good news is that wet dreams are completely normal. Wet dreams begin during puberty when the body starts making more testosterone, the major male hormone. And often they occur during a dream that has sexual images.

Although some guys may feel embarrassed or even guilty about having wet dreams, you can't control them or stop them from happening. This is because God designed wet dreams as a part of the normal sexual response—a way of preparing you to be with your future wife.

Almost all guys experience wet dreams during puberty, and many men have them as adults.

As we have discussed, as a young man, you will have strong sexual desires as you grow into manhood. If you are unmarried and keeping your sexual appetite under control, then there will be times when your "storehouse" in the testicles is overfilled. God has designed your body so that the surplus is discharged during sleep—a wet dream.

Wet dreams should be, in fact, a matter of thanksgiving to the Lord for the relief it gives you. So don't be embarrassed when you have one. Use the wet dream as an opportunity to pray and thank the Lord that he is preparing you for a potentially wonderful sexual life with your future wife.

> Rejoice always, pray continually, give thanks in all circumstances; for this is God's will for you in Christ Jesus.
>
> *1 Thessalonians 5:16-18*

Dream Land

Can you remember what you dreamed about last night? Some young men can remember their dreams in vivid detail, while others aren't sure that they dreamed at all. Dreams can occur in any of the stages of sleep, but the most memorable ones usually happen in the last stage of sleep, called REM (rapid eye movement). Even if you can't remember anything, chances are you dreamed last night as you drooled on your pillow.

Several years ago a website encouraged teens to write in about what happened most frequently in the dreams they remembered. Falling topped the list. And who can't remember a dream where they started to fall and then were jerked awake? Being in school was in the top five, which doesn't sound too exciting. Arriving too late to something was number six, just ahead of eating. Hmmm, I wonder what food they were dreaming about? Maybe a triple-chocolate sundae. Being frozen with fright came in eighth. Other frequently dreamed dreams included swimming, being naked in public, failing a test, and snakes.

You can't control your dreams, just like you can't control your wet dreams. A study in *The Journal of Clinical Endocrinology and Metabolism* found that when boys were given an extra dose of testosterone their wet dreams increased from 17 percent to 90 percent. If you're in the middle of puberty, you naturally have increased levels of testosterone, so your frequency of wet dreams may naturally increase. Research shows the average fifteen-year-old boy has a wet dream about once every three weeks, while a fifty year old man has one about every six weeks.

So while wet dreams may be an inconvenience — and a little embarrassing — rest assured, things will change.

QUESTION 24

Why is it hard for my dad to talk to me about sex?

Even if a dad knows about God's plan for sex, he still may not know how to approach the subject with his son. However, many fathers have never been taught God's view of healthy sex, so that makes it even more difficult or embarrassing to discuss this subject with his son.

The Bible says God designed sex and gave it to us as a gift to enjoy. Men can actually worship God and his design by saving sex for marriage with our wives. When a dad understands all this, then he is eager to talk to his son, throughout life, about this wonderful gift.

As you are becoming a powerful man of God, I want you and your dad to be able to discuss this very important subject. Now

I'm not talking about a one-time, sit-down, birds-and-bees talk. I'm talking about learning how to discuss very personal matters with your dad now and for many, many years to come. The conversations might include the topics like, *How to be a real biblical man, God's plan for sex and sexuality, how babies are made, pornography and its dangers, how to date or court a girl, wet dreams,* and many other topics that will challenge your thinking and behavior as you are maturing into manhood.

Undoubtedly, most dads want to talk to their boys about love, sex, and relationships. Most dads know this is a critical responsibility of being a parent, but even so, it's just not easy—for many men it's just downright uncomfortable.

One of my favorite ways to recommend that dads and sons do this is by getting away from day-to-day life for a special dad-son weekend. Going away together will help you and your dad have a comfortable environment and enough time for open discussions with each other about sex.

Ideas for this dad-son time away can be found in Family Life's *Passport2Purity*, a book and kit with materials that are designed for a father and son to do together consisting of five sessions with special projects that will help you and your dad talk about biblical sexuality. It may be one of the most memorable weekends of your life.

Another resource is *The Biblical Blueprint for Sexual Integrity*, a DVD-driven series specifically designed for parents by The Legacy Institute. The series provides the biblical framework for healthy relationships and an understanding of the divine design of men and women. It will help your dad understand how to explain what it means to be a godly man.

The Legacy Institute also has a resource called *Relationships With Integrity*, which is ideal for youth groups or small group settings. The most intimate conversations still belong with you and your parents, but these resources help you explore and express your sexuality while viewing it as a spiritual gift from God. You will find all these materials and more at www.thelegacyinstitute. com.

Now a special note for you guys being raised by single moms — especially those of you whose father is out of the picture. First of all, cheers for your mom. Being a single parent is one of the most difficult jobs in the world. She needs your full support, obedience, love, trust, and prayers. A mother can speak a lot into her son's life about respecting a woman, treating a woman properly, and loving a woman. So if your dad's not around, talk to your mom about selecting a special and very trusted man in your life with whom you can discuss these issues as you go through puberty. It may be your uncle, a pastor, a Boy Scout leader, a coach, or some other trusted man.

There are many parts of society that want to teach you things about sex that are completely false or blatantly opposed to God's plan for intimacy. Without a trusted parent or spiritual advisor, it can be very easy to become lost and damaged for life in your sexual journey.

To Dads:

> Hear, O Israel: The Lord our God, the Lord is one. Love the Lord your God with all your heart and with all your soul and with all your strength. These commandments that I give you today are to be on your hearts. Impress them on your children. Talk about them when you sit at home and when you walk along the road, when you lie down and when you get up. Tie them as symbols on your hands and bind them on your foreheads. Write them on the doorframes of your houses and on your gates. *Deuteronomy 6:4-9*

To Young Men:

> Listen to your father, who gave you life.
>
> *Proverbs 23:22*

My son, keep your father's command and do not forsake your mother's teaching. Bind them always on your heart; fasten them around your neck.

When you walk, they will guide you; when you sleep, they will watch over you; when you awake, they will speak to you.

For this command is a lamp, this teaching is a light, and correction and instruction are the way to life, keeping you from your neighbor's wife, from the smooth talk of a wayward woman. *Proverbs 6:20-24*

The Talk

For decades, when a father sat down with his son to discuss sex, it was simply known as *The Talk*. The problem is ... not a lot of fathers and sons are talking. Studies show a majority of boys learn about sex through school health classes, TV shows, magazines, the Internet, or their friends.

Unfortunately, sometimes what you learn through those sources isn't the best information. To truly understand and appreciate sex, you have to consider what God says about it in his Word.

As I explain more in the next chapter, sex isn't dirty. It's a beautiful gift from God. But sadly, many people use sex in a way that was never intended.

So when it comes to your sexuality, make sure to get your information from the best sources that you can find — and almost always that's going to be your dad (or another trusted older male) and God's Word.

If sex is so great, why should I wait?

God designed sexual activity to occur between a husband and his wife. Sex binds a couple together in physical, emotional, and spiritual ways. Having sex, or having an orgasm with someone other than your wife, although pleasurable for a moment, eventually results in intense feelings of guilt and shame. Why? Because God designed sex as a wonderful gift that is meant to be enjoyed within a marriage. Yes, sex feels good, but it's more than momentary physical pleasure. Sex is also an intimate, spiritual act, where two "become one," and it's not to be taken lightly. Your body may be physically able to perform the act, but you are actually giving a part of yourself to another person, and doing this too early, outside of marriage, can cause true, lasting, painful mental consequences, including depression, low self-esteem, guilt, and even despair.

Here's one way to think about it. Your sex drive is like a pot of water. When a fire is built under the pot, the water boils and turns to steam. Used in the right way, boiling water is a wonderful tool. But if it is misused, it can cause terrible burns and permanent scars.

Waiting can be difficult, without a doubt. Every boy will have his sexual nature awakened in him, often without warning. The highest level of this sex-drive for a boy's whole lifetime will be between eighteen and twenty years of age. Most couples don't get married until they're older, but waiting is worth it! Waiting to have sex with one person, your wife, lets you experience an incredibly close, intimate and satisfying relationship built on trust and love, and this makes the sexual experience so much more satisfying!

As Christians, we have a goal to live as God wants us to, but if you do engage in premarital sex, it is definitely still possible to achieve a satisfying and loving sexual relationship later within a marriage. However, there are potential consequences to premarital sex than can also last a lifetime. Remember, if you have sex with someone who has had sex with someone else, then it's like you've had sex with both people. In fact, you could very well be "exposed" to any number of sexual partners in this way. The more partners shared, the greater chance of consequences. Here are just a few:

Sexually transmitted diseases (STDs):

- Of the 18.9 million new cases of STDs each year, nearly half occur among fifteen- to twenty-four-year-olds.
- Human papillomavirus (HPV) infections account for about half of the STDs diagnosed among fifteen- to twenty-four-year-olds each year. HPV causes cancer of the cervix in females. HPV is also associated with several

cancers in males, including prostate, anal, and oral cancer. HPV also causes genital warts, which can be quite painful to have removed.

- Teens are much more susceptible to STDs than adults.

Teen pregnancy:

- Each year, almost 750,000 young women aged fifteen to nineteen become pregnant.
- Based on this statistic, a teenager engaging in non-marital sex has a three in ten chance of getting pregnant at least once before the age of twenty.
- Ten percent of all U.S. births are to teens.
- Teenage mothers and fathers are more likely to experience serious health and emotional problems, depression, anxiety, single parenthood, less education, poverty, and homelessness.
- Children born to teen mothers are more likely to experience health problems, abuse, neglect, poverty and incarceration (being sent to jail).

Teen abortion:

- There are usually more than 200,000 abortions per year among fifteen- to nineteen-year-olds.
- Over 25 percent of pregnancies among fifteen- to nineteen-year-olds end in abortion each year.

Recently I rode on the fastest train in the United States—from New York City to Washington, DC. This train regularly runs at 120 miles per hour and can even hit 155 mph! The reason it can go so fast is that the tracks are specially designed and welded.

Now suppose the train decided to jump off its tracks and go where it wanted to go instead of its intended course. Sure, it's no longer bound by the tracks. It's free. But the ride is no longer smooth or swift.

In fact, in just a few moments the train would be bumping along before it got totally stuck. And that is where the train would remain until it is picked up, cleaned up, and put back on the tracks.

That's the way it is with sex. God has laid down the best direction and course to take when it comes to sex. He does not want to keep you from enjoying sex, but intends for you to enjoy it maximally in marriage for the longest period of time.

Our enemies — Satan, the world, and our selfish flesh — are constantly telling us to "jump off the tracks." If we do, we'll end up stuck in the mud — dirty and going nowhere. Let me encourage you to run on the tracks that God designed for you.

Studies show the people who have the most frequent sexual activity, the most pleasing sexual activity, and the deepest and most satisfying relationships are those who are married and deeply religious. Forget what you might have seen in TV shows or in movies when singles hook up or couples live together. Those relationships are hollow, and the research backs it up. God wants you to live life to the fullest!

> Certainly … it's good for a man to have a wife, and for a woman to have a husband. Sexual drives are strong, but marriage is strong enough to contain them and provide for a balanced and fulfilling sexual life in a world of sexual disorder.
>
> *1 Corinthians 7:2 MSG*

True Love Waits

Standing alone can be difficult. Not impossible, but sometimes it can be hard to stand up for your beliefs when you're alone. You gain strength by standing together.

In 1993 the True Love Waits campaign was started to help young men and women stand together in their commitment to remain sexually pure until marriage. Lust wants things now. It doesn't want to follow God's plan for sex. But true love waits.

Right away kids got excited about banding together for purity. On June 14, 1994, 102,000 purity commitment cards were displayed at the Orlando Convention Center. A little over a month later 210,000 cards were displayed in Washington, DC, between the Capitol building and Washington Monument, with over 25,000 youth attending a rally. On that same day, students in Kampala, Uganda, organized a similar rally to encourage African youth to stay pure sexually. Through True Love Waits efforts and other education, the HIV/AIDS infection rate has gone from 30 percent in 1993 to just 6 percent in 2006.

The largest display of kids standing together for purity took place on February 11, 1996, in Atlanta, Georgia, as 340,000 cards were stacked together and raised through the roof of the Georgia Dome. Eighteen thousand kids attended the aptly named "Thru the Roof" youth rally to encourage teenagers everywhere to wait until marriage to have sex.

True Love Waits efforts are still going on today. So you're never alone in your stand and desire to stay sexually pure.

QUESTION 26

What's wrong with looking at pornography?

This question is *so* important, especially when tempting sexual images are so easy to find these days. It's crucial to know that the sin of pornography is one that many, many men — perhaps most men — wrestle with today. The decisions you make now will make a difference for many decades to come.

First of all, the Bible tells females to "dress modestly, with decency and propriety" (1 Timothy 2:9). However, society and the media tell girls (as well as boys) something different. But even if the young women in school, at the mall, or at the pool are *not* being modest, God doesn't want us to look at a woman lustfully (Matthew 5:28). Easier said than done, yes, especially when there's so much skin in plain view. Still, if you decide now to avoid looking at inappropriate images, it will be much easier to stay away from these things as you grow. It may help you to think about looking at everything through God's eyes.

The word *pornography* comes from two Greek words. The first is *porne*, which literally means *harlot* or *prostitute* (a person who sells himself or herself for sex). The second word is *graphein*, which means *to write*. In other words, *pornography* literally means *the writing of harlots or prostitutes*.

The Greek word *porne* appears several times in the Bible. In one of these instances, the apostle Paul writes:

> Do you not know that your bodies are members of Christ himself? Shall I then take the members of Christ and unite them with a prostitute [pornç]? Never! Do you not know that he who unites himself with a prostitute [pornç] is one with her in body? For it is said, "The two will become one flesh." But whoever is united with the Lord is one with him in spirit.
>
> *1 Corinthians 6:15-17*

Sexual immorality covers a broad range of sinful activities in the Bible, all of which we should work hard to avoid. Some guys may think, *"It's just a picture." No actual physical act has been committed with the person. Therefore, it's not sinful.* However, looking at pornography commonly leads to sexual acts with a real person. Jesus said:

> "You have heard that it was said, " 'You shall not commit adultery.'" But I tell you that anyone who looks at a woman lustfully has already committed adultery with her in his heart.
>
> *Matthew 5:27-28*

Some may say, *"Women are beautiful." I'm just admiring God's creation.* Sounds innocent enough, right? Besides the fact that God created that beautiful woman for her husband—not you—viewing pornography can become addicting. Like all addictions, it tends to progress toward a destructive end from seemingly innocent beginnings.

Researchers tell us that for some young men, viewing pornography can be as addicting as hard drugs. Many men who are addicted to pornography began viewing it when they were in elementary school. So remember, again, the decisions you make now will definitely impact you for the rest of your life.

Since guys are particularly stimulated by what we see, it is important to guard carefully what we allow ourselves to watch—including on TV, the Internet, DVDs, video games, and in magazines. Even some commercials are sexually provocative. Also, it's important to guard what you allow yourself to listen to, especially if it is accompanied with sexual images—as is often the case with channels like MTV.

Researchers tell us that the more you surf the Internet, the greater the chance you will be exposed to pornography. Seventy percent of fifteen- to seventeen-year-olds say they have "accidentally come across pornography" while looking for other information online. Even scarier is that 40 percent of those teens say such exposure is "no big deal."

But it is a big deal! A *really* big deal! Sexual images get implanted into your brain and will be sealed into your memory by your brain chemistry. This will affect your vision of sexuality forever.

> Flee from sexual immorality. All other sins a person commits are outside the body, but whoever sins sexually, sins against their own body. Do you not know that your bodies are temples of the Holy Spirit, who is in you, whom you have received from God? You are not your own; you were bought at a price. Therefore honor God with your bodies.
>
> *1 Corinthians 6:18-20*

> But you, man of God, flee from all this, and pursue righteousness, godliness, faith, love, endurance and gentleness. Fight the good fight of the faith. Take hold of the eternal life to which you were called.... *1 Timothy 6:11-12*

Monster on the Computer

Looking at pornographic images may seem very different than staring into the eyes of a dangerous, grotesque, massive monster. But at its core, pornography is a monster that is nearly impossible to control. One expert said showing pornography to a teen boy is like giving crack cocaine to a drug addict. The results will be devastating.

Sadly, statistics say nearly one-third of boys are frequent viewers of pornography, and nearly everybody has seen at least one pornographic image.

If you have never looked at pornography, you shouldn't think that you're weird or that you're missing something. In fact, I applaud you. You're keeping your mind clean and clear of destructive images. Because guys are so visual, once we see an image we can often conjure it up again by just thinking about it.

So when it comes to pornography, think about it as a monster. Stay away from it. Run from it. Don't think you can chain it up in the basement of your mind. It can still break free and hurt you. Instead of digging around in places on the Internet where you shouldn't go, strive to walk a clean path and honor God with what you put into your mind.

And if you do have a problem with pornography, don't wait to tell your parents. By being open and honest about your secret, you can start the healing process and shrink this monster down to size.

Pornography is a huge problem. As an industry, pornography brings in more than $100 billion a year around the world. That makes it the tenth most profitable industry on the planet behind oil, banking, drugs, alcohol, and sports. That's a sad statistic. There's no easy way to say this, so I'm going to say it to you plainly. If you're looking at pornography, you must stop now. Doing these two things today will help.

First, take a moment to pray and admit your sin to God. The Bible says:

> Is anyone among you in trouble? Let them pray.
>
> *James 5:13*

If you do admit this sin, the Bible says God is faithful and that he will forgive your sin. Not only that, he will cleanse you of all unrighteousness (1 John 1:9). Just as amazing, the Bible says God will remove your sin from you—as far as the East is from the West (Psalm 103:12).

So the first key is to seek God and keep seeking him for help, forgiveness, and power.

The second step is to find a Christian man that you trust—your dad, coach, brother, or pastor. Be sure it's someone who can keep your conversation private. Then tell them what you've been doing.

This conversation may feel a bit embarrassing. But it's something that a strong young man of God should feel very good about. Remember, part of growing as a Christian means admitting when you're wrong. It's okay to ask for help. Seek help! Get stronger!

> Therefore confess your sins to each other and pray for each other so that you may be healed. The prayer of a righteous person is powerful and effective. *James 5:16*

If you have any pornographic materials, destroy them. You and your accountability partner could get rid of them together if you would like, as proof of your personal commitment to purity. Do everything you can to keep yourself from having access to pornography. If you are having trouble with Internet pornography, then go completely offline for an agreed-upon period of time.

You could ask your accountability partner to help install a porn-blocking program, and ask him to examine your viewing history—unannounced—at any time. Have your friend set the password on the program and not tell you what it is!

Another option is to be sure that your computer, television, and any other devices that access the Internet are only used in a location where your parents can see what you are viewing.

Security software

Bsecure Online www.bsecure.com
NetIntelligence www.netintelligence.com
Covenant Eyes www.covenanteyes.com
X3Watch http://x3watch.com

If television or Internet programs are causing you problems, turn off the device. Choose what you allow to influence your mind, your heart, and your daily thoughts. Ask yourself if you would watch this particular TV show, movie, or website if Christ was in the room. Is what you're looking at and thinking about preparing you for marriage with your future wife? Is what you're doing drawing you closer to Christ and strengthening your relationship with him or harming orphan?

The answers to these questions should help you make wise decisions about pornography.

If you really want to be radical, suggest to your parents that your family go without TV for a month — or even several months. Consider it a family fast. Many people who try this end up getting rid of their sets! There are several websites that will give you some great ideas on this, including www.tvturnoff.org.

One last idea — consider starting a journal. Just purchase a blank notebook and take a few moments every day to write about what you're doing and thinking. Be sure to include your struggle with overcoming pornography. Record the times when you win over this struggle, as well as the times when you lose.

From time to time, when you read back through your journal, you'll be able to see the parts of your life of which you're pleased and the parts you're not. Figure out ways to change your thoughts and actions so that there will be more and more of the good stuff in your journal.

God gives us new, clean clothes and an entire suit of armor for protection during our spiritual battles. Read carefully what Paul says about the protection the Lord gives against sexual sin (and all sin):

> Finally, be strong in the Lord and in his mighty power. Put on the full armor of God so that you can take your stand against the devil's schemes.
>
> For our struggle is not against flesh and blood, but against the rulers, against the authorities, against the powers of this dark world and against the spiritual forces of evil in the heavenly realms.
>
> Therefore put on the full armor of God, so that when the day of evil comes, you may be able to stand your ground, and after you have done everything, to stand.
>
> Stand firm then, with:
> - the belt of truth buckled around your waist,
> - with the breastplate of righteousness in place, and
> - with your feet fitted with the readiness that comes from the gospel of peace.
> - In addition to all this, take up the shield of faith, with which you can extinguish all the flaming arrows of the evil one.
> - Take the helmet of salvation and the sword of the Spirit, which is the word of God.

So when it comes to pornography and sexual sin, you have two choices:

- You can walk by faith, believing that God's way is the best plan for your life.
- You can walk by sight, which is a dangerously misleading path to travel, especially in the area of pornography (2 Corinthians 5:7).

Your thought life is important to the Lord—and critical to your future. It will shape the man you will become when you are mature. That's why the Bible tells us:

... Whatever is right, whatever is pure, whatever is lovely, whatever is admirable—if anything is excellent or praiseworthy—think about such things.   *Philippians 4:8*

Choose to fill you mind with thoughts of the Lord and what he is doing in your life.

Be Different

According to CNBC research, every second, 28,000 Internet users are viewing pornography. Every thirty-nine minutes, a new pornographic video is being produced. And each second, $3,075 is being spent on pornography.

If you think porn isn't a worldwide problem, think again. Pornography is a monster with only one goal in mind—to control you and change your view of God's amazing gift of sex. And this monster is aimed right at you!

A U.S. government commission found that the porn industry targets twelve- to seventeen-year-old boys. Makers of porn know if they can hook you when you're young, they have a potential customer for life.

It's not easy to stay away from sexual images. You have to work hard to not fall into their trap. Take pornography seriously. Find somebody to help you stay strong. Follow the advice in this chapter, and be different. The wait is worth it!

QUESTION 28

Is masturbation a sin?

This is a question that *every* normal young man has at some time during his journey through puberty. Masturbation is simply the manipulation of the penis and genitals in a way that leads up to orgasm.

First, I want to consider masturbation from a medical perspective. There is *no* scientific evidence that indicates this act is harmful to the physical body. It does not cause blindness, weakness, mental retardation, warts on the hand, or any other physical problem. Also, if you choose not to masturbate, it will not hurt you at all — physically, emotionally, or spiritually.

Virtually all guys have masturbated. The frequency of masturbation varies from guy to guy. However, the more you masturbate, the more likely it is to hurt you emotionally and spiritually.

On the other side of the coin, the less often a guy masturbates, the less frequently he will have the desire to do so. Especially since, as I mentioned in Question 23, God has provided a natural release of the buildup of sperm through "wet dreams."

A related question I'm asked is, "If I masturbate a lot, can I run out of sperm?" No, masturbating is not usually harmful physically and will not deplete your body's sperm count. Your body continually produces sperm in a process that takes just a few weeks.

Each day a small fraction of the sperm your body produces become mature and available for ejaculation. So if you ejaculate several times over a day or two, the number of available sperm will decrease each time until the body's production has time to catch up. However, with fewer sperm, does this mean you won't get a girl pregnant? No way! Remember, it only takes one sperm to fertilize an egg.

But let's get past some of the medical questions about masturbation and head into deeper and more important waters.

Even though there are very few physical problems caused by masturbation, there can be significant emotional, relational, and spiritual effects.

One emotional effect occurs when masturbation becomes obsessive — when it is repeated over and over and becomes uncontrollable. If masturbation becomes more important than your friendships or doing your schoolwork, then it is harmful.

Another emotional effect is when masturbation causes guilt from which a young man can't escape. This type of guilt has the potential to do considerable psychological and spiritual damage.

As for the spiritual implications of masturbation, it is interesting that the Bible does not directly address the subject. There are a variety of opinions about masturbation among the few Christian writers who have had the courage to write or say something about it.

Many Christians who consider masturbation to be sinful generally believe so because it is a solo act. God intended sex to join one man to one woman in marriage. To these believers, masturbating violates this purpose. Others believe masturbation encourages young men to lust and have improper fantasies.

Other Christian authors, pastors, and physicians consider masturbation allowable—and a normal part of human sexual development. Some of these experts contend that masturbation can serve as a preparatory function for sexual intercourse within marriage. These writers also suggest that, rather than increasing sexual tension, masturbation serves to actually lower sexual tension and temptation—and that masturbation can help young men who wish to manage their sexual drive while remaining celibate.

Even though Christian authors vary on their opinions concerning masturbation, virtually all agree that the bigger issues are lust and dealing with guilt.

To be sure, sexual fantasies are forbidden for Christians. This is important since sexual fantasies are *the* fundamental issue with masturbation. Christian counselors say sexual fantasies accompanied by masturbation can become addictive and produce a destructive cycle in your heart and soul.

When it comes to sexual sin in your thought life, our media-saturated culture is always ready to pave the way. So prayer and caution are appropriate as you consider these things and make wise choices before the Lord. As men of God, it is important that we not indulge our bodies, but instead we should honor God's design for sex—physical intimacy between one man and one woman in a mutually gratifying and satisfying sexual relationship within the context of marriage.

Sexual pressures are very real and very powerful. Scripture does not condone or condemn masturbation, but the Bible does condemn sinful thoughts.

Remember, your brain is your most important sex organ. Your mind controls your sexual arousal. It has been well said, "Either man governs his passions and finds peace, or he lets himself be dominated by them and becomes unhappy."

God invented sex. He knows all about it. But God designed sexual acts to be experienced between a husband and a wife in marriage. And understand this: Jesus Christ loves you and cares deeply about your struggles. He understands them even better than you do. He will help you. Pray to him. Tell him everything you're feeling. If you are burdened by this issue, don't carry the load alone. Talk to a trusted Christian adult—such as your father, a coach, or youth pastor.

Don't allow secret sin to grow in your soul. A small seed of sexual sin may grow into a massive thornbush that makes the rest of your life miserable.

> Reflect on what I am saying, for the Lord will give you insight into all this. *2 Timothy 2:7*

> For God did not call us to be impure, but to live a holy life. *1 Thessalonians 4:7*

> … Take captive every thought to make it obedient to Christ. *2 Corinthians 10:5*

> Do not offer any part of yourself to sin as an instrument of wickedness, but rather offer yourselves to God as those who have been brought from death to life; and offer every part of yourself to him as an instrument of righteousness. *Romans 6:13*

Caring Car Ride

So how concerned should you be about masturbation? Family psychologist Dr. James Dobson has written about a discussion he had with his dad — an evangelist — on this very topic:

We were riding in the car, and my dad said, "Jim, when I was a boy, I worried so much about masturbation. It really became a scary thing for me because I thought God was condemning me for what I couldn't help. So I'm telling you now that I hope you don't feel the need to engage in this act when you reach the teen years, but if you do, you shouldn't be too concerned about it. I don't believe it has much to do with your relationship with God."

What a kind thing Dr. Dobson's father did for him that night in the family car. Of that advice, Dr. Dobson told me, "He was a very conservative minister who never compromised his standards of morality to the day of his death. He stood like a rock for biblical principles and commandments. Yet he cared enough about me to lift from my shoulders the burden of guilt that nearly destroyed some of my friends in the church. This kind of reasonable faith taught to me by my parents is one of the primary reasons I never felt it necessary to rebel against parental authority or defy God."

QUESTION 29

How can I have victory over temptation?

Without a doubt, as you grow older you will face peer pressure and times when you may consider doing something that may be harmful to your body, like smoking, drinking, experimenting with drugs, looking at porn, or having premarital sex. In addition to looking at how such actions can affect your body and mind, this book also considers "temptation" from a Christian perspective and how your choices can affect your faith and your relationship with Jesus Christ.

First of all, curiosity is natural and normal. It's normal to wonder about trying a cigarette when you hear about it happening with other kids. It's normal to think about sex when you're bombarded by images everyday on television, in magazines, on the Internet, in school. In fact, temptations exist all around you, and they will be there every day of your life. Being tempted to sin is part of human nature. That doesn't make us bad people, even if we succumb to temptation. But the better informed you become and the more you learn about the changes your body is going through, the better prepared you will be to make well-informed choices. Being aware of what's out there can give you discernment, or good judgment, a gut-feeling kind of reaction that can help you determine if something you may want to do is right or wrong, or if a situation should be completely avoided.

Think about what is important to you right now. How do you want to live? What kind of character do you want to be thought of? Do you want to be thought of as an athlete? A good student? A caring and considerate person? Do you want to stay away from drugs and alcohol or save yourself until marriage? Deciding in advance how you want to live can help you stand strong, even when your friends may think differently.

As Christians, we believe our bodies are a temple, a way to worship God, and God wants us to remain pure. Does this mean that if we mess up God won't forgive us? Absolutely not! But several "Truths" may help you when temptation strikes.

Truth 1: God may test us. He may allow trials to purify and strengthen us, but he does *not* lead us into sin. In our culture, people commonly blame their mistakes on peer pressure, leaders, parents, upbringing, genetics, or any number of other culprits. As long as you look for someone or something else to blame, you will be totally helpless in combating temptations.

In fact, Jesus himself was tempted in every way, just as we are, and he suffered when he was tempted, so he knows what it's like, and it's good to have him as our defender! (Hebrews chapter 2)

Truth 2: Everyone faces temptation. None of us is tempted in some new or unique way. While we are each completely unique, the temptations we confront are basically the same ones that have confronted all men throughout history.

Truth 3: The Bible tells us that when we are tempted, God won't let us be tempted more than we can stand, and God will provide an escape route (1 Corinthians). The tricky part is choosing to follow that escape route, which could mean turning off the computer, avoiding certain books, movies, or friends, or sometimes escaping can mean literally running away!

Yes, this can be easier said than done. But there are steps you can take to escape temptation—besides running away!

1. **Pray.** When tempted, quickly pray to God about what you're experiencing. These on-the-spot, lightning-quick prayers allow you to ask your Father in heaven for grace and strength to avoid the temptation—and to take the way of escape he has provided.

2. **Read scripture.** No matter what happens in our lives, the Bible gives us a guide to live by. God's Word gives us rules and advice to help in every situation. Even though the events described in the Bible happened thousands of years ago, its words of wisdom are just as relevant today. Plus, memorizing and reciting scripture can help during times of temptation. Think about your favorite scripture when your thoughts turn negative. The Word of God is powerful. Jesus used scripture to rebuke Satan when he was tempting Jesus in the desert. And remember, when you are tempted, God won't let the enemy tempt you more than you can stand. God will provide an escape route.

3. **Avoid temptation in the first place.** Don't put yourself in situations where you know you will be tempted. That greatly increases your chances to mess up! If you start dating, go on group dates. Avoid friends who encourage you to watch movies you know your parents won't allow—or tell them in advance you won't watch it. On several occasions, Christ told his disciples to pray that

they might not fall into temptation (Matthew 6:13; Luke 22:40).

4. **Encourage one another.** Since we are not uniquely tempted, we can help, support, and learn from each other. As Christians, God wants us to help each other and build each other up in our faith (Ephesians 4:15-16). Having a small group of guys who can talk and pray together can be critical in avoiding various sins which so many young men fall into.

5. **Confess.** When you fall, remember you can pray and ask for God's forgiveness and strength to avoid the temptation the next time.

How can a young person stay on the path of purity?
By living according to [God's] word.   *Psalm 119:9*

I can do all this through him who gives me strength.
                                              Philippians 4:13

When tempted, no one should say, "God is tempting me." For God cannot be tempted by evil, nor does he tempt anyone; but each person is tempted when they are dragged away by their own evil desire and enticed. Then, after desire has conceived, it gives birth to sin; and sin, when it is full-grown, gives birth to death. Don't be deceived, my dear brothers.
                                              James 1:13-16

Strong Roots

I'm not a dendrologist, a person who studies trees and certain plants, I'm a doctor. But I want to share something I have learned about the coastal redwood tree.

Coastal redwoods are the tallest trees on earth. The tallest grew higher than a football field is long. The tree measured 367 feet, while a football field is 360 feet long (including the end zones). This tree was also an amazing forty-four feet around at its base!

So what does a tree have to do with encouraging others and finding people who will help me avoid temptation? A lot actually. While coastal redwoods grow to huge heights, these trees have very shallow root systems. Their roots only go four to six feet deep and spread out more than one hundred feet. These redwoods are able to survive terrible winds and rains by growing close to each other and interlocking their roots to strengthen each other. By supporting each other, redwoods live thousands of years and become the mightiest of all trees.

Finding good friends and mentors will help you stand strong when facing the temptations of teen years. Think about what makes friends "good." Do they encourage you or put you down? What do you talk about together, watch and read? Where do you hang out? Is your friend a believer? Good friends help each other grow stronger in your faith, and they make life more enjoyable. So put down roots with your Christian friends and grow some lives that stand out for Christ.

QUESTION 30

When will I become a man?

For nearly two decades, I spent time at local public schools answering the questions asked by fifth-grade boys about puberty, their changing bodies, and sex. One of my favorite questions was, "When will *I* become a man?"

I usually turned the question around and asked it of the fifth graders themselves. Here are a few of the most common answers:

- When you get married.
- When you get hair on your body.
- When you have sex the first time.
- When you get your first car.
- When you go to college.
- When your dad says you're a man.

I enjoyed listening to their answers and then surprising them with my response. According to the Bible, you become a man in God's eyes around the age of twelve.

When I said this, the eyes of the boys would become as wide as saucers. Maybe yours are also.

There's a story in the Bible about a very young man named David. The Lord chose him when he was still a boy. Even though his mind, body, and spirit were not yet fully mature, God considered him a man. And the Bible says that the Spirit of the Lord was upon David in power (1 Samuel 16:12-13).

Even so, when David volunteered to fight Goliath, one person said, "You are only a young man" (1 Samuel 17:33). Even Goliath mocked David's youth. Yet this young man defeated Goliath — and Israel defeated the Philistines.

Another example is seen in the life of Jesus. Do you remember the story of Jesus being taken to Jerusalem when he was twelve? On the way home, the family realized Jesus was missing. When they returned to the city, they found Jesus sitting with the priests in the temple.

Jesus told his parents that he had to be in his Father's house doing his Father's business. Even though Jesus's body wasn't fully developed — even though he was probably only just entering puberty — God still directed Jesus to do something that only "men" normally did — teach in the temple — during a time that he was still growing mentally and physically (Luke 2:41-52).

So a completely mature body is not required for you to be looked upon as a man by God. Your body and mind may still have some growing and maturing ahead, but I would like to say welcome, young friend, to manhood! Even if others say that you are not a young man, in God's eyes you are. You are a young man who has been designed, exactly as you are, by a God who loves you more than you can ever imagine.

Jewish families celebrate a Bar Mitzvah when a boy is thirteen years old to recognize the transition from boyhood into manhood. At the Bar Mitzvahs I have attended, the Rabbi has taught several truths from the Bible:

- Before creation, God had a plan for you and your life. To God you are not a surprise. You are totally unique. There never has been, nor will there ever be, another you.
- You have been uniquely designed physically and mentally. God did not make a mistake in your design.
- From this day forward, you will be held accountable as a man. You will no longer be treated as a child. You must begin to act like the man that you are.

Despite the fact that God considers you a young man — it is critical for you to understand the character traits of a real man. These traits must be learned and practiced. To be a real man of God, even a young man, means that you have become responsible for obeying God's rules and his call in your life. A real man of God realizes that rules and limits are designed for his protection, and he obeys his parents and teachers. Young men of character work hard to get along with their parents.

Real men follow rules and do the right thing, even when parents and teachers are not around. They appreciate and honor their parents.

A real man is honest. He keeps his promises. He works hard at his schoolwork and chores and takes care of his clothes and his room and of all things entrusted to his care.

Real men are loyal and trustworthy. They support their friends. They serve and respect others. Real men respect and honor the girls and women in their classes, their neighborhoods, and their families.

Real men are careful about their minds. They avoid immoral or sexually provocative pictures, movies, and books.

And real men wait until marriage to have sex. They promise to God, their wife, their family, and their friends that they will do everything they can to remain married to one person for life.

Real men learn to read the Bible and spend at least a few quiet moments talking with and listening to God every day. They commit to memorizing the Word of God. Men of character understand that church may not always be fun, but they attend regularly with their family. They love and support their pastor and church leaders.

Finally, a real man learns to know his own heart, feelings, and desires, and he learns to be real — sharing his inner feelings and thoughts with others. He also learns to be aware of and to respect the feelings and thoughts of others. A real man learns to live at a deeper level.

A real man is strong and courageous. He protects and provides for and leads others with strength and love. A real man of God sacrifices himself for those whom God has entrusted into his care.

How does a young man do all this? By walking with Jesus, the ultimate real man, by submitting to him (his lordship and his will), by listening to him (by reading and memorizing his word and listening to him in prayer and quiet time each day), and by learning from him.

So when do you become a man? In God's eyes, you are! You're a young man, but nevertheless, a man. Now it's time to begin acting like a young man of God. Now it's time to choose whether you will be a run-of-the-mill man, or a real man — God's man.

If you choose the latter, the Bible promises you will have a life that is full of "love, joy, peace, forbearance, kindness, goodness, faithfulness, gentleness and self-control" (Galatians 5:22-23) — a life that is richly satisfying. In short, this is a true call to manhood. You will be blessed and will be a blessing to many.

> Be on your guard; stand firm in the faith;
> Be courageous; be strong. Do everything in love.
>
> *1 Corinthians 16:13-14*

Trust in the Lord with all your heart and lean not on your own understanding; in all your ways submit to him, and he will make your paths straight.

Do not be wise in your own eyes; fear the Lord and shun evil.

This will bring health to your body and nourishment to your bones. *Proverbs 3:5-8*

Whatever you do, work at it with all your heart, as working for the Lord, not for human masters, since you know that you will receive an inheritance from the Lord as a reward. It is the Lord Christ you are serving. *Colossians 3:23-24*

But seek first his kingdom and his righteousness, and all these things will be given to you as well. *Matthew 6:33*

Becoming a Man

In many cultures the transition from boyhood to manhood is marked with a test or ceremony. Some are celebratory in nature, like the Jewish Bar Mitzvah, others, well, involve some pain.

- In East Africa among the cattle-herding culture of the Barabaig, young men go through a manhood ceremony where their head is shaved bald and three deep cuts are made in their foreheads that go from ear to ear. This often leaves permanent "manly" scars.
- On the South Pacific island of Vanuatu, every spring large wooden towers are constructed that often reach more than one hundred feet in the air. Men climb the tower, tie vines to their feet, and dive off headfirst. Divers can reach speeds over forty miles per hour before the vines catch and jerk them to a stop. Amazingly, the

goal of the jumper is to hit the ground with his shoulders before the vines catch him. Land diving dates back more than fourteen centuries. Boys as young as five years old take part in this rite of passage. Young boys start by jumping from low heights. But as a boy gets older, he goes higher and higher up the tower. The higher the point that a man jumps off, the manlier he is considered by the tribe. (I guess bungee jumping is considered for babies on Vanuatu.)

- Becoming a man in the Hamar tribe of Ethiopia is much less dangerous. Instead of the cow jumping over the moon, you have to jump over the cow. Actually, the young men in the Hamar tribe have to run across the backs of a herd of cows three times. In a long and sometimes painful ceremony, the tribe forms a circle around the cows. The young boy comes to the ceremony naked, jumps onto a bull, climbs to his feet, and starts running on the backs of the cattle. When he makes it across three times, all the tribe shouts and the boy is now a *maza* (man).

- In the Brazilian Amazon rainforest, the Satere-Mawe tribe uses bullet ants in its manhood ceremony. Ever heard of a bullet ant? Well, they're sort of like a fire ant on steroids. Bullet ants can be nearly an inch long and their sting is considered one of the most painful on the planet. If you think a wasp sting is bad, it's nothing compared to the sting of a bullet ant. One person described it as causing "waves of throbbing, all-consuming pain that continues for up to twenty-four hours." The Satere-Mawe carefully sew more than one hundred bullet ants into a ceremonial glove that goes halfway down the forearm. To become a man, a boy must stick his hand into the glove and endure painful stings for over ten minutes without making a sound. Sounds horrible, right? Well, it's not over. Boys can go through this ritual several times (even up to twenty) to achieve a high rank in the tribe.

In much of the Western world, including the United States, Canada, and Europe, there isn't a clearly defined rite of passage from boy to man. But don't let that be an excuse to continue to live immaturely and not take on the responsibilities of being a man. Talk to your parents about coming up with your own ceremony to mark your transition into manhood. Just make sure to mention to them to keep away the ants.

APPENDIX A
Accurately Measuring Your Height and Weight

To record an accurate height and weight for yourself, here's the technique recommended by the Centers for Disease Control and Prevention (CDC):

Measuring Your Height Accurately at Home

1. Remove your shoes and bulky clothing.
2. Take the height measurement on flooring that is not carpeted and against a flat surface such as a wall with no molding.
3. Stand with your feet flat, together, and heels against the wall. Make sure your legs are straight, arms are at your sides, and shoulders are level.
4. Make sure you are looking straight ahead and that your line of sight is parallel with the floor.
5. Have someone else take the measurement while you stand with your head, shoulders, buttocks, and heels touching the flat surface (wall). Depending on your overall body shape, all points of your back may not touch the wall.
6. Use a flat headpiece to form a right angle with the wall and lower the headpiece until it firmly touches the crown of your head.
7. Make sure the measurer's eyes are at the same level as the headpiece.

8. Lightly mark where the bottom of the headpiece meets the wall.
9. Then, use a metal tape (that won't stretch) to measure from the base on the floor to the marked measurement on the wall to get your height measurement.
10. Accurately record the height to the nearest eighth of an inch.

By the way, did you know you are actually taller in the morning? At night the discs (little cushions) between your vertebrae swell and you might be a quarter to a half inch taller in the morning than at night! Try it!

Measuring Your Weight Accurately at Home

1. Use a digital scale. Avoid using bathroom scales that are spring-loaded.
2. Place the scale on firm flooring, such as tile or wood, rather than carpet.
3. Remove your shoes and clothing. It's okay to keep your underwear on.
4. Stand with both feet in the center of the scale.
5. Record the weight to the nearest decimal fraction (for example, 55.5 pounds).

APPENDIX B
Height for Age Growth Chart

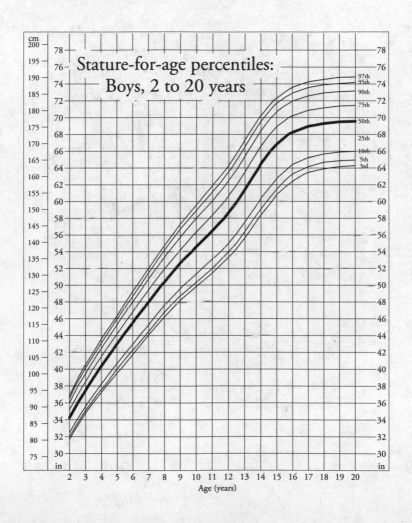

Stature-for-age percentiles:
Boys, 2 to 20 years

APPENDIX C
BMI Percentile Chart for Boys

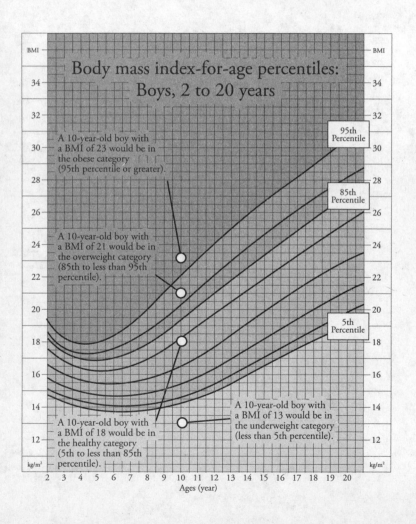

Body mass index-for-age percentiles: Boys, 2 to 20 years

A 10-year-old boy with a BMI of 23 would be in the obese category (95th percentile or greater).

A 10-year-old boy with a BMI of 21 would be in the overweight category (85th to less than 95th percentile).

A 10-year-old boy with a BMI of 18 would be in the healthy category (5th to less than 85th percentile).

A 10-year-old boy with a BMI of 13 would be in the underweight category (less than 5th percentile).

95th Percentile

85th Percentile

5th Percentile

BMI

kg/m²

Ages (year)

AFTERWORD

I'm thankful to a volunteer panel of expert advisors who spent considerable time reviewing virtually every draft of the manuscript and have, with their corrections, advice, and wisdom, made it much more accurate and reliable:

- **Counselors/Psychologists:** David Armentrout, PhD (Tulsa, Oklahoma); Ed Dawson, MS (Lexington, North Carolina); and Gerry Weitz, BA, MA (Colorado Springs, Colorado).
- **Dermatologist:** Kim Dernovsek, MD (Pueblo, Colorado).
- **Educators/Youth Specialists:** Carrie Abbott (Kenmore, Washington); John Fuller, MA (Colorado Springs, Colorado); Scott Guttery (Ft. Myers, Florida); Kate Larimore (Colorado Springs, Colorado); and Beth Vogt (Colorado Springs, Colorado).
- **Family Physicians:** Brian Duignan, MD (Easton, Massachusetts); Susan A. Henriksen, MD (Glen Rock, Pennsylvania); Gaylen M. Kelton, MD (Indianapolis, Indiana); Don Nelson, MD (Cedar Rapids, Iowa); Mary Anne Nelson, MD (Cedar Rapids, Iowa); Dean Patton, MD (Greenville, North Carolina); J. Scott Ries, MD (Bristol, Tennessee); Rob Vogt, MD (Colorado Springs, Colorado); and Mari Sanchez Wohlever, MD (Orlando, Florida).
- **Internists:** Ken Dernovsek, MD (Pueblo, Colorado), and Leanna Hollis, MD (Blue Springs, Mississippi).

- **Pediatricians:** J. Thomas Fitch, MD (San Antonio, Texas); Ed Guttery, MD (Ft. Myers, Florida); Kim Jones, MD (Los Altos, California); and Paul R. Williams, MD (Pisgah Forest, North Carolina).
- **Psychiatrist:** Todd Clements, MD (Plano, Texas).
- **Young Men:** Nate Henriksen (Glen Rock, Pennsylvania), Jason Ries (Bristol, Tennessee), and David Wohlever (Orlando, Florida).
- **Theologians/Pastors:** Larry Miller, DMin (Baton Rouge, Louisiana); Sammy Tippit (San Antonio, Texas); and Gerry Weitz, BA, MA (Colorado Springs, Colorado).
- Appreciation is also due to another panel of experts who volunteered to read one or two initial drafts and/or the final manuscript for medical and theological accuracy:
- **Counselors/Psychologists:** Dwight Bain, MA (Orlando, Florida), and Les Parrott, PhD (Seattle, Washington).
- **Educators/Youth Specialists:** Melissa Cox (Denver, Colorado), Scott Guttery (Ft. Myers, Florida), Karen Harmer (Indianapolis, Indiana), and Barb Larimore (Monument, Colorado).
- **Family Physicians:** Matthew Acker, MD (Almaty, Kazakhstan); Ruth A. Bolton, MD (Mankato, Minnesota); Mitch Duininck, MD (Kabul, Afghanistan); Julian Hsu, MD (Denver, Colorado); Adam Myers, MD (Dallas, Texas); Kent Petrie, MD (Vail, Colorado); Edward E. Rylander, MD (Tulsa, Oklahoma); Raja Saade, MD (Ft. Worth, Texas); Laurel Williston, MD (Tulsa, Oklahoma); and Jacob M. Wood, MD (Ruston, Louisiana).
- **Pediatricians:** Diane Foley, MD (Colorado Springs, Colorado); Annelise Spees, MD (Colorado Springs, Colorado); and Joseph Zanga, MD (Columbus, Georgia).
- **Young Men:** Garrett Bain (Orlando, Florida), Logan Cox (Denver, Colorado), Levi Duininck (Kabul, Afghanistan),

Elijah Myers (Dallas, Texas), Scott B. Larimore (Atlanta, Georgia), John Leslie Parrott (Seattle, Washington), Josh Rylander (Tulsa, Oklahoma), and Stephen Spees (Colorado Springs, Colorado).

- **Theologians/Pastors:** Robert R. Fleischmann (Hartford, Wisconsin); Dave Flower, MA (Monument, Colorado); Alan Harmer, ThM (Indianapolis, Indiana); Gerald Parsons, MDiv (Waxahachie, Texas); J. V. Thomas (Cape Town, South Africa); Sammy Tippit (San Antonio, Texas); and Rodney Wood, DMin (Baton Rouge, Louisiana).
- Thanks also to the Christian Medical and Dental Associations (particularly David Stevens, MD; Gene Rudd, MD; and J. Scott Ries, MD) for providing an in-depth review of the final manuscript. Appreciation is also due to my longtime legal and business counselor and friend, Ned McLeod.

I'm thankful to Kathleen Kerr at ZonderKidz for the trust she extended to me in asking me to write this book—and to Jesse Florea and Jacque Alberta applying their considerable skills in shaping and improving the manuscript. Nevertheless, any errors remaining are my responsibility and should not be taken as a reflection of the many people and resources on which I relied as I wrote this book.

I'm most thankful to God for calling me into the unmatched privilege of being his child. I pray that this book will bring honor and glory to him, his name, his kingdom, his Word, his Son, his Spirit, and his church.

Walt Larimore, MD
Monument, Colorado
February 2011

NIV Boys Bible

Grow into the young man God wants you to be. Dig deep into God's Word and discover inspiring people, stories, and all kinds of stuff you never ever imagined was in the Bible.

Features include:

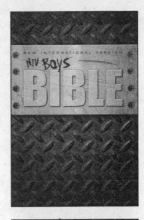

- Grossology—Gross and gory stuff you never knew was in the Bible
- What's the Big Deal?—Need-to-know biblical stories and people
- Check It Out—Fun facts about Bible times and characters
- Makin' It Real—Apply Bible stories to your daily life
- Hundreds of highlighted verses worth memorizing
- Introductions to each book of the Bible
- Presentation page
- Complete NIV text

Available in stores and online!